MW01621229

A Child in the Midst of Battle

One Family's Struggle For Survival In War-torn Manila

To Kathleen & Jerry,
Never forget - Tora, Tora, Tora.
We have known each
other since we were teenagers,
Kathleen and now this
book will tell you about
my life before we met.
With warm regards,
Evelyn Berg Empie
2010

Published by Satori Press, 904 Silver Spur Road #323, Rolling Hills Estates, CA 90274 USA. First edition. First printing.

Printed in Hong Kong.

ISBN 0-9617268-8-1

Library of Congress Cataloging-in-Publication Data is available

A Child in the Midst of Battle

One Family's Struggle For Survival In War-torn Manila

Evelyn Berg Empie
and
Stephen H. Mette

with original watercolors and drawings by Xavier Aboitiz

for my grandchildren,
and for their grandchildren

Contents

Foreword

Manila, the Philippines—once known as the "Pearl of the Orient"—was one of the most heavily damaged cities in World War Two, second only to Warsaw, Poland. During the culminating Battle for Manila, the Imperial Army retreated through the city, pushed toward Manila Bay by advancing American military forces. In their wake the Japanese left a charred swath of almost complete destruction, fulfilling their mission to leave the city "stone upon stone."

An estimated 180,000 civilians were killed in the war, more than died in the nuclear holocaust of Hiroshima and Nagasaki combined. Philippine civilians and Allied military personnel alike suffered unspeakable atrocities at the hands of Japanese soldiers. Their stories are legion, but largely unknown to the outside world.

At this dawn of the Third Millennium, the Japanese government has yet to apologize for, nor even acknowledge, their actions in the Philippines during the second Great War. It is my hope that the testament which follows will in a small way open the eyes of an uninformed world.

Evelyn Berg Empie
April, 2001

DESDE LEJOS NOS MIRA

One: Invasion

overleaf—title reads: "From far away He watches us"

That day was to go down in history as *a day of infamy*—December 7, 1941, the day the Japanese attacked Pearl Harbor. Not many Americans realize that Manila was also bombarded that same day. But because the Philippines was on the other side of the International Date Line, it was December 8th for us. My sister Elyse and I were at a party celebrating the First Communion of our cousin, Tony Rocha. I was almost ten. Elyse had just turned seven.

The party was held on the top floor of a "highrise," which in those days was probably only four or five stories tall. One of the guests left early, but quickly returned.

"*¡Los Japoneses han bombardeado Hawaii!*" she cried frantically. "*¡Muchos muertos en la base naval!*"

An eerie silence settled over the room. It was disbelief, perhaps, or suspicions confirmed, as grown-ups had been whispering about the possibility of war.

The party quickly dispersed. Elyse and I went outside. People rushed by on the street with frantic determination. Our driver, Irineo, drove us to the Army & Navy Club on the esplanade of Manila Bay where my parents, Fé and Ernest Berg, were attending a wedding.

We turned the corner and saw them waiting anxiously for us outside the club. When mom saw that we were unharmed she clapped her hands in a prayer of gratitude. Her shoulders slumped as if she were exhaling for the first time in several minutes.

We drove home in silence. Imperial warplanes swarmed in the sky. Bombs fell like dark rain on nearby air fields and ships in the harbor. Ordnance smoke drifted across the water. Some of the ships carried Christmas goods for sale in the local stores. Dad—who owned a department store called Berg's on the fashionable Escolta Boulevard—lamented that his Christmas order was at the bottom of Manila Bay.

When we reached home, Mom put us girls—Elyse and me, and our sister Elaine, then three years old—under the heavy dining room table of Philippine mahogany in hopes that it would protect us from flying shrapnel. We were terrified, and prayed the rosary ever so fervently. Dad stood in the doorway watching fighter planes engaged in dogfights over the city.

I crawled out from under the table and stood beside him. American P-38s and Japanese Zeros twisted in the sky in a dangerous chase. Bombs fell to ground in a hail of smoke and debris. Mom screamed at me in panic until I crawled back under the table. She pleaded with dad to join us, but he just looked at her sadly and shook his head.

"There's no point, Fé," he said, "we don't stand a chance. There aren't enough soldiers to defend the city. The Americans will surrender, and the Japanese will march right in."

Dad was right, and not for the last time. As a child he had survived World War I in Germany. Instinctively he knew what lay ahead of us.

Fierce bombing continued throughout December. Japanese warplanes dropped their loads of destruction on the city at every time of the day and night. The *ack-ack* of antiaircraft fire was deafening. Tracer bullets shredded the night sky. Whenever we heard planes overhead we scurried into a large closet beneath the stairs.

Day after day we held our breath at the sound of bombs whistling through the air—a horrible sound you don't forget—and braced for explosions that rocked the earth. Ardently we prayed for the poor Americans soldiers who received the brunt of the attack.

I don't know what the fighting was like for the soldiers, but for we civilians it was surreal. Set against a backdrop of fearsome daily battle, our lives continued pretty much as they had before the invasion—Irineo drove dad to work, and Elyse and me to school. Mom ran the house and visited with friends.

But where before the canvas of life had been cast in hues both idyllic and mundane, it then was stained the color of human viscera, brushed with violence. At any moment, the fighting might crash down around us. If luck was with us, we made it to a shelter in time. If luck was with us, we were protected from harm.

I went to school at Assumption Convent, which was operated by a French order of nuns. We students often had wondered what lay beyond the doors at the head of a particular wing of the school which was off limits to us. Soon the air raid sirens wailed, and we found out.

The sisters ushered us into a long interior hallway which led to their quarters, and told us to sit quietly on the floor. We huddled there in the dark for what seemed the longest time. We were protected well enough by the massive stone walls of the convent, yet still could hear the shells exploding outside. The nuns told us the Japanese were only bombing military installations, but it sounded to me as if the whole city was being razed.

Late in December, General Douglas MacArthur, commander of US Army forces in the Far East, acknowledged that his troops were insufficient to repel the Japanese offensive. American and Filipino forces retreated west across Manila Bay to Corregidor Island and the Bataan Peninsula. After pledging his return, MacArthur boarded a boat with his wife and son, and a few close aides, bound for Australia. No one thought it would take him three long years to make good his promise.

We spent Christmas Eve, 1941 in the shelter beneath the stairs. Dad had lined the little room with mattresses and pillows to make it as secure and comfortable as possible. Mom cursed the Japanese for picking that particular night to bomb the city nonstop.

Elyse and I worried about Santa Claus maneuvering his sleigh through enemy aircraft. Dad assured us that Santa was a miraculous being, and would find his way unharmed through the shelling. What a welcome relief it was to worry about Santa for one night instead of whether a bomb would destroy us where we lay. Finally we slept, albeit not with "visions of sugar plums" dancing in our heads.

Christmas morning dawned clear and quiet. We ran upstairs to our bedroom to see if Santa had made it through as promised. The previous night we had placed our shoes on the window sill, a custom of my father's native Germany. There to my wondrous surprise I found my very first wrist watch, a beautiful gold timepiece with a black grosgrain band. Oh, Joy! And on the floor beneath my shoes was a lovely doll dressed in a nurse's uniform. I was so grateful to Santa for braving enemy bombers to bring us our gifts.

On January 2, 1942, the Americans declared Manila an "open city," and ceded it to the Japanese. With no effective resistance in place the Imperial Army marched right in, as dad had predicted. Many of the soldiers entered the city by foot and on bicycles. We were conquered by men on bicycles! The adults worried about the possible horrors that awaited us. I imagined columns of monsters marching through the streets.

Huge banners were unfurled on the sides of buildings proclaiming "Asia for the Asiatics." Billboards were rewritten with Japanese ideograms. The Rising Sun replaced the Stars and Stripes on flagpoles around town. We were instructed to click our heels and bow to any Japanese soldier we passed on the street. Disrespect was swiftly and harshly punished.

Stores and schools reopened. We were instructed to continue our lives as if nothing had changed. Propaganda of all sorts exhorted us to be grateful for our liberation from the grips of American imperialism, an irony not lost on the locals.

Our daily routines returned to normal, but everything was different. Each morning before class we had to face in the direction of Japan, and with arms outstretched yell the *banzai* salute as the Rising Sun was hoisted up the flag pole. We were taught to read and write Japanese, and learned Japanese history. Imperial Army officers arrived at school unannounced to make sure we were learning what they wanted us to know.

Text books were confiscated. All passages dealing with the United States were blacked out. Even the peso sign replaced dollar signs in math books. It was very distracting to open a text and see black spots all over the page.

Military rallies were held in a large park called the Luneta. Often we were pulled from class and made to march single-file through the sweltering streets of downtown Manila in our starchy uniforms. We stood for hours while generals and other officials gave speeches. In Japanese, of course—we didn't understand a word of it.

The rallies lasted so long we brought lunch and ate standing up, something new for us as we were used to going home for a hot meal and *siesta*. I pitied the nuns who were forced to stand for hours in the noonday sun in their neck-to-ankle robes and constricting head gear. I don't know how they managed.

The German occupation of France produced a large local quisling population. But little if any collaboration occurred in the Philippines. Stories had filtered back to us early in the war of atrocities committed against American and Filipino soldiers on the Bataan Death March. Overtly the local civilian population acted as the Imperial Army instructed. But in our hidden hearts we hated the Japanese, and did what we could to aid the Allied cause.

Two: Before the War

overleaf—413 Dakota Street, Manila, c. 1930:
the author's birthplace

My childhood memories before the war recall a way of life much like the one described in *Gone With The Wind*. As in the American South, the heat and humidity in the tropics was an oppressive physical presence that slowed the pace of life to a crawl.

The houses had high ceilings and large windows with sliding *capiz* shell shutters that opened for maximum ventilation. To accommodate the monsoon flooding, houses were built several feet above the ground on wooden stilts or thick stone pilings. It was relatively cool beneath the house, and we kids loved to play under there.

Spain ruled the Philippines for four hundred years. After the Spanish-American War (1898), the Islands became an American protectorate. Decades later, class distinctions were still deeply rooted in Spanish colonialism. Many of Spanish decent, members of my own family included, considered themselves of an elite caste. The indigenous population was discriminated against in ways both subtle and obvious. For participation by some in my family in a culture of exclusion, I apologize.

So-called racial purity was a vital consideration when choosing a mate. As with many European royal families, the available gene pool in Manila was only about ankle deep. Everyone knew each other, certainly, but many of us were also related, by marriage if not blood. A lot of my schoolmates were second- or third-cousins.

We had a cute little Fox Terrier named Trixy, and a pet mongoose named Patsy, who scampered up the curtains and along the top of the curtain rods. Mom slithered a fabric measuring tape on the floor like a snake. Patsy crouched and stared intently at the tape, gauging its distance, before finally pouncing on it.

Each of us girls had her own nanny, called a *yah-yah*, until we were old enough to go to school. *Yah-yahs* were local Filipina girls. They were sweet and nurturing, and became very attached to their young charges. Our *yah-yahs* kept our rooms clean, folded our clothes, picked up our toys, and saw to it that we finished our meals. Mom was preoccupied with our diets, always saying "Eat!"

A laundress picked up our laundry each morning, pounded it on a rock in the Pasig River, and ironed every single item, including underwear and sheets. Two houseboys cleaned upstairs and down. They glided across the hardwood floors like ice dancers on *bonotes*, or coconut fibers, which worked as buffing agents to shine the inlaid wood floors.

The Berg girls before the war (from left): Evelyn, Elaine, Elyse

Our cook, a chubby, jovial woman named Consuelo, went food shopping twice a day. Sometimes I went with her. The market was an open air affair with fruit and vegetable stands. Consuelo moved adroitly through the crowd with a large wicker basket on her arm. I struggled to keep up with her. It seemed I was always bumping into people.

Fresh cuts of meat were laid out in the open. Proprietors waved off the flies with shreds of paper attached to a stick. Once I saw a slab of meat that was so fresh a muscle was still twitching.

Consuelo bought live chickens and beheaded them in the kitchen. She plunged the birds into boiling water to facilitate the feather plucking. One day I saw a headless chicken bounding about the kitchen. Yuk! From then on I made sure to stay away when I knew we were having chicken.

In the tropics everything shuts down during the hottest part of the day. After lunch came *siesta*. As with children everywhere, Elyse and I rebelled at the specter of sleeping when it was light outside, thinking ourselves too mature. Instead we played. We designed clothes for our dolls, attended make-believe parties, and immersed ourselves in games of all sort. Our favorite doll was a paper doll named Beverly, only with our Spanish accents we referred to her as "Beaver-ley."

One stipulation for not taking a nap was our absolute silence so dad could sleep. One afternoon we got rambunctious. Soon we heard his footsteps coming down the hall. Dad wore slippers made of glove-soft leather which slapped on the hardwood floors when he walked—*slap, slap, slap.*

We heard him coming and knew we were in trouble. He spanked us on the rump with his slipper, a loud whack that startled more than hurt. Our egos took more of a beating than did our fannies. Dad sent Elyse to one corner of the den, and me to another. We were to face the wall and stay put until he woke up.

Of course it didn't take us long to tee-hee at each other across the room. Soon we were sliding around on the floor in our stocking feet, having a grand time. All without speaking a word or making a sound.

Then came the slippers again down the hall—*slap, slap, slap.* We thought we had somehow been found out; mom and dad seemed to have a certain radar for knowing when we misbehaved. Back to our corners we slid, and stood at perfect attention. But this time no spanking. Dad released us from our penance.

Elyse and I played Hopscotch on the walk in front of the house. Six years my junior, poor Elaine was usually left behind with her *yah-yah.* Mom often pleaded with us to let Elaine join in our games of Kick the Can or Hide and Seek. "Let her be *salingpusa*," mom always said. This is a hard word to translate into English. In this context mom meant, "let Elaine think she is playing even though she really isn't, and what she does doesn't count for anything."

Street sellers passed through the neighborhood offering their wares. A Chinese man in a straw coolie hat and rubber soled slippers often ambled by. He sold *ampao*—sugary treats of puffed rice—from baskets that dangled from a bamboo bar slung across his shoulders. He called out, *"ampao...! ampao...!"* his baskets swaying back and forth as he walked.

Sometimes the *ampao* man would put down his baskets under the big rubber tree in our front yard and chat with us as he wiped his brow. One of us girls would run to the kitchen to get him a glass of water. He told us his Chinese name, but to us it sounded like "Jimmy," so we called him Jimmy Ampao. He told us that he had attended a culinary school in Europe, and had worked as a chef in a fine hotel restaurant in Shanghai. He spoke English with a British clip, and had a good vocabulary.

Fé in traditional Mestiza dress

When the Japanese plundered China they killed his family. Somehow he managed to escape unharmed. Eventually he found his way to the Philippines, where he lived in a single room, wore tattered clothes, and sold *ampao* on the street. Later, Consuelo was recalled to her home province for a family emergency. My parents bemoaned her loss. That's when I told them about Jimmy.

Dad loved the finer things of life; he was thrilled to have a gourmet chef preparing our meals. Jimmy Ampao was happy to be in a home with a nice family. Everybody won. Dad taught Jimmy to make German pea soup and *wienerschnitzel.* Jimmy introduced some wonderful dishes to us.

When food became scarce later in the war, Jimmy Ampao created innovative dishes from what few ingredients were available. He proved to be a loving and faithful servant. Through all our wartime travails he stuck with us the remainder of our time in the islands.

Ernest Berg

Dad was a merchant, born and bred. By the time war broke out he had a large department store on the fashionable Escolta Boulevard in downtown Manila. Whenever I meet old-timers from Manila they excitedly tell me that Berg Escolta is where they went to buy outfits for special occasions.

I was fascinated with dad's store, and often went there to look at the merchandise. By the age of seven, dad figured I was old enough to try my hand at selling. During winter break from school he put me in charge of the Christmas card section. I had to climb up on a stool in front of an old fashioned pot-bellied cash register to ring up my sales.

Dad also founded a company called Red Star Auto Stores. By the early 1940s, he had built a chain of thirty-two stores throughout the islands. His supplier was

Western Auto Supply, which was based in Minneapolis. Dad's American business partners sent us wonderful Christmas gifts. One gift I especially remember was a pair of sterling silver candlesticks, which mom managed to save when our house was destroyed, and graced her dining room table to the end of her life.

In the days before the Internet people spent a lot of time together. We enjoyed a rich family and social life. Air-conditioning had only recently been introduced in Manila. Ours was one of the few local families fortunate enough to have it, though only in a couple of rooms and then only for part of the day.

After dinner we congregated in the gloriously cool den to play games or read. We all loved to read. One entire wall of the den—floor to ceiling and wall to wall—was lined with books.

While the men attended to the affairs of business and state, the women went shopping and hosted *meriendas*, or mid-afternoon tea parties. *Meriendas* meant animated conversation and plenty of sweets.

To ward off the heat, the ladies carried ornate fans that made clicking sounds when they were opened and closed. The more excited the conversation became over the latest bit of gossip, the louder and faster the fans clicked.

Dad wondered how, with all the women yakking at once and the fans madly clicking, the ladies ever heard each other. Yet when *merienda* was done, everyone was current on the latest scuttlebutt—they hadn't missed a word.

My mother was raised to be a wife. She succeeded or failed at womanhood based on the quality and position of her husband. Her job was to see to the children's upbringing, run the home, and host the occasional cocktail- or dinner-party.

Mom was only nineteen when she married. Dad was twenty-eight, self-possessed and worldly beyond the mere difference in their ages. His word was law, and she acquiesced to his every command. Not to say they didn't love and respect each other—I think they did. That was just the nature of the world in which they lived, and neither one of them questioned their place in it.

Most weekends found a party at one house or another. When it was mom and dad's turn, the house became a hive of activity. The servants did the actual work, of course. Mom's job was to bellow orders and worry. Reputations were at stake. Tactical strategies of music and menu were poured over like battle plans.

When the servants had been properly set to task mom pulled herself together, a surprisingly complicated operation. There was the frenzied, last minute gown fitting—the parties were strictly formal—the hair and makeup, and just the right kind and amount of perfume. It was a grueling job, but mom was a trooper.

Late afternoon was crunch time. Mom issued a last-minute barrage of orders, then disappeared into her bedroom. It was eerily quiet in there. I wondered what she was up to. I cracked open the door and peered inside. The windows were shuttered, the room was dim.

I found her lying on her back on the floor with her feet on the bed and cucumber slices on her eyes. The elevated feet gave her cheeks a rosy glow, she explained. Cucumber slices kept her eyelids from being puffy. Just two of the beauty secrets that have passed down in an unbroken chain from mother to daughter in my family for a long time. Maybe for as long as there have been cucumbers.

I looked forward to my parents's parties the way I anticipated Christmas—eagerly and for weeks in advance. The night of the big event I was overwrought with nerves. As darkness fell, stately black cars lined up down the block. Liveried chauffeurs deposited their charges on the front walk.

Elyse and I sneaked out of our room and sat on the second floor landing with our legs dangling through the banister stiles, watching the guests arrive. The men were dashing in crisp linen suits. Every woman's gown seemed to outshine the last. To my young eyes it was the height of sophistication. I dreamed of the day when I would take my place among them.

Once arriving couples had made their entrance, the women pealed away from their husband's sides to "freshen up," which amounted to gossip and cosmetic damage control.

Houses at that time had only one bathroom. Ours was on the second floor at the top of the stairs. Elyse and I would huddle outside the door and listen to the patter. The dresses were big and poofy from an overabundance of crinoline and silk taffeta. When the women moved, their dresses made loud *shushing* sounds like the rustling of dried leaves. What a racket!

When I was nine I made a new friend. I discovered her sitting in the branches of a mango tree in the backyard, partly hidden by foliage. She called herself Elizabeth. It was an exotic sounding name to me, as all my friends had Spanish names.

Elizabeth was about my size, with light brown hair that fell to her shoulders. She wore a filmy pastel dress and went barefooted. The most interesting thing about her was a rather large pair of gossamer wings.

Elizabeth began popping up when I least expected her: on top of the china cabinet, or on a curtain rod with her legs dangling down. We always smiled and said hello to each other. My friend Mari Lu Rodriguez bemoaned the fact that she couldn't see Elizabeth. Elyse doubted her existence.

"I'll have to see her to believe her," she said.

We spent our summers in Baguio, a mountain resort a hundred miles north of Manila. At several thousand feet in elevation, Baguio always seemed cool, a welcome relief from the heat and humidity of the city. We prepared for our vacations months in advance by ordering sweaters from the Sears catalog. Mom was convinced we would need them.

Dad worked in the city during the week and came up on the weekends. Mom put rouge on our cheeks in anticipation of his visits. She said it was cold in America, and all the children there had rosy cheeks. Dad must have shaken his head.

We spent a lot of time outdoors. I loved the feel of the cool air on my cheeks, and the exotic scent of pine trees. The mountainous northern region of the Philippines, on the main island of Luzon, was the only place in the country where pine trees were found.

Elizabeth came on vacation with us the first year I knew her. Elyse was exasperated about her inability to see my fairy companion. One day I asked Elizabeth when Elyse would be able to see her. "When you're nine, like me," I told Elyse, relaying the answer. I also told her that Elizabeth would leave candies in the yard so that Elyse could be sure she existed.

During *siesta*, when I was certain that Elyse was asleep, I got down my piggybank and quietly took out some change. I ran down to the *sari sari* store on the corner and picked out some hard candies from the large apothecary jars that they had on the counter. *Sari sari* stores were little markets like today's convenience stores. They commonly had a thatched roof made of palm fronds, or *nipa*.

Fearing that Elyse would awaken before I finished my task, I ran home breathless and hid the candies in some *copa de oro*—cup of gold—flowers in the backyard.

I sneaked back into bed and pretended to wake up when Elyse did. She squinted at me with a look of profound mistrust.

"I suppose there's candy in the yard," she said.

"I don't know," I said, "let's check."

I followed her outside and watched her searching the

flowers. I'll never forget the look on her face when she spotted the candies.

Eventually I outgrew Elizabeth. Or maybe it was the other way around. Three years later, Elyse anticipated her ninth birthday with more excitement than usual. Finally she would get to see Elizabeth. She was crestfallen when I told her that I had made it all up.

"But the candies..." she lamented.

Another summer in Baguio I happened upon a portly Caucasian man sitting on the front steps of a house with an open briefcase propped on his knees. I didn't encounter a lot of people who looked like my dad. Curiosity got the better of me.

I approached the man and struck up a conversation. He introduced himself as Mr Cassel. His accent was thick but recognizable. Not only did he look like dad, he sounded like him too. I surprised Mr Cassel by asking if he was German. He told me that he was a German Jew. He and his wife and young daughter had barely escaped the Nazi purge. They fled the country with virtually the clothing on their backs.

Back home he had been a business executive. After reaching the Philippines, he secured a position as a sales representative for an American pen and pencil manufacturer.

When dad arrived later in the week he called on my new friend. It turned out that Mr Cassel had been the general manager of a large department store in Germany, and that his wife had managed the women's department. Dad wasted no time hiring both Cassels to manage Berg

Escolta.

A lasting personal and business relationship developed, followed them to the United States after the war, and lasted all the rest of their days. Mr Cassel credited me as a vital link in the chain of his destiny, and always held me in a special place in his heart.

Our connection to Baguio was renewed each winter when our Christmas tree arrived. We decorated it with fragile glass ornaments that my parents had purchased on trips to Europe in the 1930s. Dad's mother sent holiday boxes from Germany packed with colorful ornaments, and small candles that clipped on to the tree branches. Our efforts were accompanied by raspy carols blaring out of our big Victrola. Elyse and I took turns placing the fragile black records on the turntable and cranking the handle.

After dinner on Christmas Eve, we lit the candles. The flickering lights reflected off the glass ornaments giving the room a magical glow. Mom played carols on the piano, and we all sang along. Dad always had tears in his eyes. Perhaps he was thinking of his childhood long ago in a homeland far away.

Three: War Declared

We lived near Manila Bay in the Paco/Ermita district of central Manila. In the days and weeks following the invasion, our grandmother, Carmen Romero Mandelbaum—Mamita, or "little mother," to us—took Elyse and me out to Dewey Boulevard, commonly called the Bóule, which ran along the esplanade. We sat on the massive boulders that fronted the harbor and listened to waves gently lapping against them. The sunsets, for which the Philippines is famous, were magnificent.

In surreal juxtaposition to the idyllic setting, battles raged twenty-five miles across the bay on Corregidor

Island and the Bataan Peninsula. Clouds of battle smoke rose over the water. When a big gun fired we heard its muffled report. The sound of the guns was eerie, frightening. We prayed fervently for the Americans soldiers who fought to save us.

Decades later, I finally learned what happened in those battles. On our 1983 trip to the Philippines, my husband Richard and I took the 45-minute hovercraft ride to Corregidor, an island in the mouth of Manila Bay which had been a fortress under Spanish rule. The Japanese had totally destroyed the island. Four decades later all that was left were the ruins of what had been a thriving military base, a ghost town memorial to what had been.

A couple of families lived on the island as caretakers. One of the men was certain that the island was haunted with the souls of American and Filipino soldiers who had died there. He told me that over the years many people had seen what appeared to be ghosts roaming the grounds, had heard what sounded like troops marching and cries in the night.

A tour bus drove us around the island. Our guide recounted the story of the American defense of Manila in 1941. After the invasion, American and Filipino troops retreated to the island to consolidate their men and supplies. There were days when the island was bombarded continuously for twenty-four hours. Allied troops returned fire, but ultimately were outgunned.

There wasn't a dry eye on the bus when we encountered the spot where the Rising Sun replaced the Stars and Stripes. General Jonathan Wainwright surrendered his troops on May 6, 1942, five months after the invasion. Ten thousand U. S. and Filipino soldiers were later forced on the dreadful Bataan Death March to concentration camps in Cabanatuan.

At first it appeared as if, in surrendering, General Wainwright had betrayed the United States and his men. But when MacArthur liberated the camps at Cabanatuan in 1945, he shook hands with Wainwright, who wept openly upon seeing his commander. MacArthur told Wainwright that he had put up an heroic fight at Corregidor, but that surrender had been inevitable.

I shall never forget walking through the Melinta Tunnel on Corregidor, where American soldiers had holed up after retreating from Manila. The tunnel was like an underground city, with a series of lateral shafts containing offices, a mess, and even a hospital. Through the years I have heard from several sources, mostly military men, about a mysterious apparition seen by many the night before the American surrender.

It rained that night. The camp was thick with mud, heaping misery on the men's already bleak mood. Though desperately hungry and weak, they had been unable to sleep knowing that in the morning they would be sent to concentration camps.

Late in the night a lovely woman was seen walking amongst the men offering words of encouragement and inviting them to pray. Many thought her a nurse from the hospital in the tunnel, but none could recall seeing her before. The lady's presence brought a measure of peace to the camp. Finally the men slept.

The following morning some of the soldiers went to pray at a local chapel. They gasped in astonishment at what they found there. On the altar was a small statue of the Blessed Virgin Mary. The statue's feet were muddy, its face unmistakably that of the woman they had seen the night before. The priest asked the men to carry the statue in a procession.

I have been told by many independent sources that during that somber ceremony, it rained rose petals from the sky, an odd occurrence certainly, and especially so since roses don't grow in the Philippines—it's too hot.

While people of Japanese descent were being interned without cause in the United States, so too were the Japanese detaining American and British citizens in the Philippines. Makeshift camps were set up on the campus of Santo Tomas University, north of the Pasig River in the Santa Cruz district of Manila. Mom's father, Francis "Cheri" Mandelbaum—Papito to us—was one of many arrested, his only crime being that he was American. It was sad to see him locked up like a criminal.

Papito's son, mom's brother Freddie, also was interned at Santo Tomas. Before the war Freddie had graduated from the University of Southern California and returned home to marry Carmen Rickards. By happy coincidence Freddie ran into a school friend, Dan Golenternek, at a Jai-Alai match in Manila before the war. Student Dan had become Doctor Dan, a U. S. Army medical officer serving in the Philippines. Later they were interned together at Santo Tomas, where their friendship deepened.

Early on we were allowed to visit family members at the camp. We signaled to Papito from the wrought iron fence that circled the campus, and slipped him fresh fruits and medicines through the bars. Soon the Japanese hung grass matting on the fence, and we could no longer see inside. The American Red Cross delivered "care packages" to the camp, but they never reached our loved ones.

Overcrowding at Santo Tomas was horrendous. The elderly and/or the infirm, Papito among them, were relocated to Remedios Hospital, a medical facility hastily established on the grounds of Malate Catholic Church near our home. We blew Papito kisses from the street; he waved to us from a second-floor balcony.

A second camp called Los Baños opened up on the outskirts of the city, but did little to relieve the abysmal conditions. After several months Philippine-born internees with one non-American parent were released. Freddie qualified. But as the enemy—or perhaps only half an enemy—he wasn't allowed to hold a job. Freddie and Carmen sold their wedding gifts piece by piece to get by. Freddie traded commodities on the black market. Eventually Carmen's jewelry went too.

Dad's pride and joy was a shiny new 1941 Ford convertible. It was a magnificent machine. Irineo had charge of the family car, but only dad drove the Ford. He often took us out for Sunday spins along the waterfront. Convertibles were a rarity in Manila. Heads turned wherever we went.

After the Japanese had established control of the city, all private automobiles were confiscated and shipped to Japan. It broke dad's heart to turn over the keys. After the cars were gone, the prevalent mode of transportation became a two-seater horse-drawn carriage called a *carretela*. Irineo then had horses to feed instead of gas tanks to fill. Our backyard became a horse paddock.

Dad purchased a beautiful golden Arabian stallion, which he named Pomeroy, from a man who had played polo before the war. Pomeroy was a spirited beast. He often pranced about the yard as if still on the field of play. I had a horse named Patience. Elyse had Florian, a piebald stallion. Mom didn't like to ride, but little Elaine had a pony she called Spinach.

Private radios soon went the way of the automobile. The Japanese didn't want the locals to know how the Americans were faring in the war. They confiscated our radios and altered them to receive only certain stations playing propaganda.

Many people kept illegal—unaltered—radios, and secretly listened to broadcasts from Hawaii. News spread through an underground pipeline. It was dangerous to keep such radios. Many people were killed when their radios were discovered.

In the years before the war there were two kinds of people in Manila: those who did, and those who did not play mah jong. Mom did not, but Freddie's wife Carmen was an avid player. Back then the tiles were made of bone, or perhaps ivory. What a racket they made when they were shuffled on the table.

Carmen's husband Freddie had a friend with an

illegal radio. The men sometimes met under the house to listen to Allied broadcasts. Upstairs the ladies made as much racket as they could with their mah jong tiles to cover the sound of the radio. This activity lasted only a short while—it was very dangerous.

Mom's good friend, Bebé McMicking, continued listening. Bebé was married to an American interned at Santo Tomas. Bebé herself was from an old Spanish family, and so was allowed to take her four children to live with her parents. She listened to Hawaiian broadcasts in secret, and relayed information to her husband through the wrought iron fence before the matting went up. The news spread quietly throughout the camp, lifting the spirits of the internees.

One day Bebé stopped coming to visit. It wasn't until after the war that her husband found out why. The Japanese had discovered her radio. They marched into the parents's home, and slaughtered Bebé, her children, her parents, and all of their servants.

My father, Ernest Berg, was the oldest of six children from the small textile manufacturing town of Bocholt outside of Cologne, in Western Germany near the Dutch border. His father, Mathias, was a textile engineer who married a Dutch woman named Wilhelmina Wiggers.

The onset of World War I shattered the tranquility of Ernest's rural home town life. Mathias went off to war. Ernest, a young teenager, was spared the draft. As the eldest son he assumed responsibility for the family. Food was scarce. He often had to sneak across the Dutch border late at night on his bicycle to collect produce from Wilhelmina's farmer relatives.

Mathias survived the war, but soon after was killed in a motorcycle accident. The family fell on hard times. Ernest quit high school and took a job at a local textile mill. Having to work while his friends went to school embarrassed him. He switched to the late shift to avoid running into his classmates.

It soon became apparent to Ernest that there wasn't enough of a future in the German textile industry to satisfy him. He had bigger plans, and decided to move to America. He and his brother Alfred crossed Europe and Asia on a motorcycle with a sidecar.

Wilhelmina must have been beside herself with fear at the prospect of her two oldest boys leaving home on a motorcycle, especially so because her husband had been killed on one.

To help finance the trip, Ernest sent written accounts of their adventures to the hometown newspaper. Two and a half years later, he and Alfred caught a freighter in India bound for the United States. But when they steamed into Manila Bay, Ernest was so taken with the warm tropical setting and the beautiful sunsets—or perhaps only because he had run out of money—that he postponed his passage to America for two decades.

As dad's little girl, I knew him only as a stern but also loving and playful father. But I have since formed a mental picture of my father as an adult male and businessman based on the impressions of his friends and colleagues.

By all accounts Ernest Berg was a commanding presence. Physically he was only of average height, but had a striking appearance: white-blond hair, crystalline blue eyes and a deep tropical tan. Ernest had the confidence and bearing of a man who knew what he wanted, and knew how to get it.

To a person, everyone I have talked with who knew my father called him foremost a take-charge guy. When he entered a room, one would automatically sit up a little straighter. There was never a doubt who was boss.

And there was substance behind the façade. Ernest's mind was restless, always working, looking beyond the next couple of curves in the road. He had forward-thinking ideas, and the drive and competence to realize them. His department store, Berg's, catered to the middle class. Nothing unusual there. But he placed it on a prominent street corner on the fashionable Escolta Boulevard, Manila's version of Rodeo Drive. Regular people loved "shopping up," and flocked to Berg's.

Dad also noticed a business opportunity in auto parts distribution. When cars broke down, it wasn't unusual to wait a week or ten days for the parts to arrive. Dad created a web of auto parts stores which significantly reduced the time required to obtain auto repairs. It seems an obvious solution today, perhaps, but at that time, in that place, the idea was revolutionary. Investors lined up down the block to give dad their money.

But underneath it all, I have been told and have experienced directly, Ernest Berg was first and always a family man. Everything he did, he did for his family.

If Ernest was the serious one, brother Alfred had an

eye for the señoritas and liked to party. So while Ernest put his nose to the stone, learning the local languages and beginning to build his empire, Alfred had fun. He briefly dated Elisa Ugarte, mom's best friend since kindergarten, and together they arranged a double date for Ernest Berg to meet Fé Mandelbaum.

One fateful evening Elisa and two German gentlemen called at Fé's house. They were installed in an informal living room at the top of the stairs—what today would be called a family room. Fé would be along, they were told, as soon as she finished her piano practice.

Ernest courting Fé (at left), with Alfred Berg and Elisa Ugarte, c. 1928

Many times through the years, dad recounted the story of the beautiful music he heard coming from another part of the house. So drawn to the music was he, that after a moment's hesitation he descended the staircase in search of its source.

In the formal living room at the foot of the stairs he discovered a tiny young woman at a baby grand piano, her feet barely reaching the pedals. Her fingers seemed to float above the keys, creating what he called "music from the gods."

Sensing another presence in the room, her eyes lifted from the music. What they beheld was as unusual a physical presence as might be found in the Far East: European features, white-blonde hair, striking blue eyes. He seemed to her an exotic creature.

That may have been the moment they fell in love.

Dad foresaw the battle for the liberation of Manila when it was still years in the future. Figuring we would be safer outside the city, he purchased a country house near the town of San Francisco del Monte, about an hour's drive northeast of the city. By horse-drawn carriage, or *carromata*, a larger version of a *carretela,* the trip took half a day or more. Dad kept a skeleton staff there to grow fruits and vegetables, and raise chickens. He built us a tree house out of bamboo.

Pomeroy and Spinach were left at the country house, as was a new horse called Merry Legs, so named because of a big white star on its front hoof. Dad and his girls loved to ride, often venturing far and wide in the outlying countryside.

My sense of direction was never the greatest. I always got lost, which drove dad nuts. He decided to teach me to have a good sense of direction. I'm not sure how he thought he could do that exactly, but his plan was a simple one. When it was time to return home from one of our extended rides, dad galloped off, leaving his daughters to find their way home alone.

Well, I never had a clue which way was which. I was always scared to death. My only salvation was Patience: I let go of the reins, and she got us home. Dad was always waiting for us when we trotted into the yard. He congratulated me on a job well done. I never let on that Patience deserved all the credit.

Four: An Occupied People

The Japanese were strict disciplinarians when it came to order in the city. Civilians were forced to adhere to a stringent set of rules, regulations, and policies. We had to walk quietly with our eyes averted, had to bow and politely greet every Japanese soldier we encountered.

Behind their backs we thought them crude and hateful. We called them *Taparrabos*—Spanish for g-string—for their practice of cooling themselves in the spray of curbside fire hydrants wearing only straps around their genitals.

Infractions of the rules were not tolerated. We were loath to draw the attention of even the lowliest foot soldier, lest we incur his wrath for some arbitrary offense. Filipinos caught stealing or misbehaving were beaten and often killed on the spot, usually before an audience.

One afternoon Elyse and I were walking with Mamita on Escolta Boulevard. We and several other pedestrians were ushered into a circle around a Filipino man who was lying on the sidewalk. I don't know what the man did, but as we watched a soldier bayoneted him to death. We were not allowed to flinch, or to cry out or show any emotion whatsoever.

It pains me to think of it now, as I've tried to keep it on the back burner of my mind all these years. But every once in a while certain stories creep out of the depths of my subconscious.

Another time, Elyse and I again were out with Mamita. I remember a chain link fence, with a huge expanse of lawn beyond it. Perhaps it was a government building. On the lawn was a Filipino man tied to a cross. He was moaning, "*tubig… tubig…,*" which in Tagalog means "water."

Who knows how long the man had been hanging there. When the Japs had their audience, they thrust a hose down the man's throat, and turned on the water full force. Then they turned the cross upside down.

Despite the growing number of such incidents, mom and dad tried to keep our daily lives as routine as possible. Schools were on the European schedule, which meant Thursdays and Sundays off. After school on Wednesday, Irineo took Elyse and me to Mamita's house to spend the night, as he had done before the war. Mamita always had a surprise for us. I remember a doll bed with a beautiful hand embroidered quilt, and pillows of organdy and lace. Another time she hand-sewed a dress for my Betsy Wetsy doll.

After dinner Mamita sat us down on the hardwood floor in her bedroom. Unadorned with rugs, the floor was the coolest spot in the house. Carefully she brought out her holy cards one by one from the bottom drawer of her armoire. The cards were her treasures, tiny works of art imported from Italy and Spain, individually wrapped in tissue paper. Some were made of lace. Most had a relic attached to the card in a cellophane envelope: a tiny piece of thread from a saint's robe, a strand of hair, or a bone fragment.

Carmen Romero Mandelbaum (Mamita)

Mamita told us the story of each saint, including any gory details of death by torture for refusing to renounce their Christian faith. As a young child I knew more about the lives of the saints than I did about even the most common fairy tales.

Thursdays, Mamita took us out into the world. We went to a movie, or out for shopping and lunch. During the early war years the stores were still open, selling whatever merchandise was available. Sometimes we were lucky enough to find toys for sale. Mamita read the manufacturing labels on all the packages, and got excited when she found one made in the USA. "Oh," she would say in her Spanish accent, "it's from 'oosa'."

Sometimes we went to Chinatown which sold goods from all over Asia. Mamita wrinkled her nose if the word "Nippon" was stamped on an item. We picked up hand-carved fans smelling of camphor, or perhaps a new pencil box. For some reason I loved pencil boxes. Some had a secret panel. A lot of those same items are still sold in shops in Chinatown today. I smile when I see them.

We loved going to the movies. Since the supply was limited, we had to see the same ones over and over again. We didn't mind. Beside loving the movies themselves, they were shown in air-conditioned theaters, still an unusual phenomenon in those days.

We were introduced to a new character called Mickey Mouse, who appeared in a short animated film called *Steamboat Willie.* We saw Shirley Temple movies, always my favorites. Abbot and Costello made Mamita giggle. There were Nelson Eddy and Jeanette McDonald musicals, which put me in a dreamy mood. I hoped that I would one day find a man to love me like that. Deanna Durbin flicks made us dance and sing when we got home. But we never saw Westerns—those were for boys!

The movie that had perhaps the biggest impact on me was *The Thief of Baghdad.* I believe I only saw it once as a child, but it had a lasting affect. It wasn't until my grandsons Nathan and Timothy were born that I purchased a video cassette of the film. The boys were hooked on it for the better part of a year. Every time they came to visit they had to see it.

The huge, ugly spider in the film didn't have the impact on them that it had on me. The movie's hero, Sabu, entered a giant stone statue through its nostril, and encountered the spider in a shroud of fog. Sabu cut the web. The spider plunged into a watery pit, where it was devoured by an octopus. For years I was terrified of that spider. Many a night I tucked in the mosquito netting around my bed as a matter of self-preservation.

One day soon after seeing *The Thief of Baghdad*, Elyse and I noticed a huge spider web spanning the branches of two mango trees in Mamita's backyard. Square in the middle of the web was an ugly black spider, its body the size of a wine bottle cork, the legs big and hairy. That spider freaked me out; it never moved. It gave me the willies just thinking about it. I had to find a way to get it out of there.

Elyse and I each filled a bucket with rocks and took them upstairs. We sat on the window sill in Mamita's bedroom, dangling our legs through the wrought iron grill, and threw rocks down at the spider. Sometimes one of us would rattle the web, but the spider never moved. It was so frustrating. After a while, our arms were so limp from throwing rocks that we could only drag up one bucket of rocks between us.

After the movies, Mamita took us for ice cream and cake at a restaurant on the top floor of one of the highrise buildings on the Escolta. Adjacent to the restaurant was a radio station. A glass wall allowed us to watch disc jockeys talking into microphones and playing records. Sometimes they would come around the tables to interview us.

Often we stayed home for lunch. Half an hour before eating, Mamita would stand on her tiptoes—she was only 4'-10"—and reach way up onto the top shelf of her china cabinet, and come down with three aperitif glasses. She ceremoniously poured each of us a tiny bit of sweet vermouth in a glass to help whet our appetites.

Mamita had traveled extensively in Europe, Asia, and the Americas. She kept her worldly trove in a glass china cabinet in the family room at the top of the stairs. One of her mementos was a delightful orchestra of tiny porcelain frogs from Germany, each one playing a different instrument. I was so fascinated by the amphibian ensemble that periodically I pestered Mamita to give them to me.

Finally she relented. But not until I turned sixteen, she said. That would be her gift to me. Oh, joy! For years I ticked off the months in my mind, waiting impatiently for my sixteenth birthday. I wonder if I would have enjoyed the frogs half as much had she just given them to me. Or was the anticipation my greatest delight?

Today, my granddaughter Elizabeth likes to look in my glass cabinet, much as I did fifty years before her. I have a snow globe with Heidi's mountainside cottage. (*Heidi* is Elizabeth's favorite Shirley Temple movie.) Elizabeth shakes the globe, and watches the snow fall. When she asked me if she could please take it home with her, I told her indeed she could… when she turned sixteen.

May is designated the month of the Blessed Virgin Mary in the Catholic religion. Thursday afternoons in May meant an extra church service. Girls carried baskets filled with flowers for the Benediction. Elyse and I wore white dresses, and headbands adorned with flowers. At one point in the service we would go up to the altar, and, while singing a song to the Blessed Virgin, throw flowers at her statue. I always felt special after these services.

We also completed the Novena of First Fridays, which promises that Last Rites will be administered before death. On the first Friday of nine consecutive months, Mamita took Elyse and me to mass and Holy Communion before school. Completing a Novena is a real commitment, and more difficult to accomplish than one might imagine. I always felt the Sacred Heart of Jesus within me on those Fridays, and felt a real sense of accomplishment after it was done.

Filipina women were usually stationed outside the church. They sat on their haunches, cooking on earthen pots called *kalanes.* Their specialty was *bibingka*, a pancake-like breakfast bread wrapped in banana leaves. They tasted good with a big cup of hot chocolate. Mamita shaved chocolate into a pot of hot milk, and twirled a wooden hand mixer between the palms of her hands, creating a frothy topping. It was so good.

We also had *suman* for breakfast, sticky rice cakes shaped like tiny pillows wrapped in banana leaves, steamed before eating. After peeling back the leaves, we sprinkled sugar on top, and dipped the pieces in the hot chocolate. Luckily for me Los Angeles has a large Filipino population. I have access to bakeries offering *bibingka*, *suman*, and other native delicacies. But somehow it all tasted better as a child.

Papito's father, Frederick Mandelbaum, was born in Sulzbach, Germany, in 1838. As an adult Frederick became a banker. In the mid-1860s, his employer transferred him to St. Thomas, in the Virgin Islands. There he met and married Celina de Sourdis. He was twenty-six, she but thirteen.

Growing up I had always been told that the de Sourdis family was French-Catholic. Later I learned that Celina's paternal grandparents had been Jews living in Spain during the Spanish Inquisition, which ended in 1820. To avoid persecution, the grandparents took the name of a local priest named de Sourdis who helped them escape across the Pyrenees Mountains into France. Celina's father Jacob was born there soon after.

Frederick's bank again transferred him, this time to Barranquilla, Colombia. Francis (Papito) was born there, the third of four children. Five years later, Frederick died of liver trouble at the age of thirty-eight. Celina, in her mid-twenties at the time, moved her children north to Detroit, Michigan to live with her sister Rachael.

Francis "Cheri" Mandelbaum (Papito)

Celina nicknamed Francis after her father's middle name, Cheri, a French diminutive meaning "cherished one." After high school Cheri matriculated at Cornell University in upstate New York, where he studied architecture and played shortstop on the school baseball team. His teammates once carried him off the field on their shoulders after he had made a game-saving play. After graduation, Cheri took a job building homes for coffee plantation workers in Guatemala. He was well-liked by his co-workers, who called him Panchito.

After the U. S. victory in the Spanish-American War (1898), the Philippines became an American protectorate. The United States, in a move to upgrade Manila's infrastructure, put out the call for working professionals. Seeking to gain additional experience before returning home to the United States, Cheri accepted a two-year position as an architectural draftsman.

He rented a room in a Manila boarding house owned by a widow named Felisa Romero. At night Cheri and the two or three other tenants took their meals with the family. The eldest of Felisa's three children was a girl named Carmen, just twelve or thirteen years old at the time.

Two years quickly passed. Cheri lingered in Manila. And even though he had saved a couple of pesos by that time and could afford his own place, he stayed on at the boarding house. For as had his father before him, Cheri had fallen in love with an adolescent girl. But whether for reasons of finance or social convention, he waited until she turned the advanced age of eighteen before asking for her hand in marriage. Literally he watched her grow up.

Cheri ended up living in Manila for four decades. Such was the allure of the Romero women. Cheri became a well-respected architect in his own right. He built many of the grandest buildings in prewar Manila: the Post Office, City Hall, Philippine General Hospital, as well as schools and homes for the rich. He also held the position of Professor of Architecture at Santo Tomas University.

I naturally assumed I would marry and grow old in the Philippines, and couldn't wait to show my children and grandchildren Papito's work, and tell them stories about the sweet, wonderful old man who was my grandpa. I couldn't know then that a few short years later the retreating Imperial Army would raze the city, in the process destroying much of his life's work.

Mom's first cousins were the Rodriguez children; eight of them. The kids were closer in age to Elyse and me, so we always considered them our cousins more than mom's. Whenever we spent a long weekend at the San Francisco del Monte house we were allowed to bring a friend or two. Many times it was one of the Rodriguez kids.

The Rodriguez family had owned a grocery store in central Manila which had burned to the ground. They moved north across the Pasig River to the Quiapo district, and opened up a new store called El Canal de Suez.

The father, Marcelino, hung tripe to dry in the basement, and made the most wonderful Spanish sausage in the islands. His reputation reached far and wide. Apothecary jars filled with penny candy were situated on the counter near the cash register. We always got to pick some when we went for a visit.

In order to recoup his losses from the fire, Marcelino ordered a shipment of Muscatel wine from California to supply Catholic church services throughout the islands. Being such a Catholic country, one can only guess how many churches there were in the 7,000 islands that comprise the Philippines.

Marcelino anticipated a tidy profit from the wine, but his timing couldn't have been worse: the ship from California arrived at the same time as did the Japanese invasion.

American naval forces diverted inbound merchant ships to the Visayan island group in the central part of the Philippines. With the ships went Marcelino's order. Someone must have had a heck of a party with all that wine. Marcelino and his family had a big struggle ahead of them, but like life itself, eventually everything worked out.

Merchant ships tied up in the harbor had all been sunk when the Japanese invaded. The bottom of the bay was loaded with cargo. It didn't take long for enterprising locals to dive down for the merchandise. All over Manila one could see makeshift tables set up with a small array of goods: a few bottles of ink, new pots and pans, some perfume; whatever had been salvaged from the holds of the sunken ships. No doubt dad's Christmas order ended up on someone's table.

I wanted to set up a table in front of our house. Dad asked me if I was planning to dive into the bay with the other salvage crews for merchandise. When I gave him an emphatic "No!" he took me by the hand to one of his Red Star Auto stores. He "loaned" me twenty pesos to purchase whatever I thought I could sell. He explained profit and loss, and made it clear that after the goods were sold I had to reimburse his original investment. Any money left over was mine to keep. Profit: what a concept.

I set up shop in front of Mamita's house. Filipinas often walked the streets selling wares from baskets they carried on their heads. I purchased some tomatoes and fresh fruits from some of these roving merchants. I priced my items a little higher—that was my profit—and I sat…

And sat.

Then I sat some more.

Hey, I'm not making any money, here. What's the problem?

Mamita sensed my discouragement, and asked what I would charge for the whole lot. She assured me that she really needed everything I had for sale. I worked up a price, not forgetting that I owed dad twenty pesos. After an awful long wait for my first sale, I was suddenly out of business in a matter of minutes with a tidy profit jingling in my coin purse.

Later I went into the thread business. My mother's cousin Pilar, also called Piluchi, was a talented seamstress. Many fashionable ladies opted for her gowns and dresses. Somehow I got a hold of some spools of thread, and let Piluchi know that I was in business. Whenever she called with an order, I delivered the items on bicycle. Eventually my supply ran out. Piluchi took to unraveling socks for thread. One gets creative during a war.

After private vehicles were confiscated, there wasn't much use for dad's auto parts inventory. He hired local seamstresses to manufacture *bayongs*—fabric satchels with handles—out of automobile seat cover material. The *bayongs* were more convenient for food shopping than were the open wicker baskets, as they were pliant and shielded meats and fruits from the tropical sun. Dad's *bayongs* were an instant hit, and started popping up all over town.

THE HEAVENS ARE THERE, AND YOU ARE LOVED.

X.A. 3/97

Five: The Dark Descent

Mom was deathly afraid of running out of food. Soon after the Japanese invaded, I found her digging in the garden. She didn't like to work in the yard, and as a pianist she was always protective of her hands. But there she was on her knees in the dirt, sobbing, pulling up all the flowers and replacing them with vegetable cuttings and seeds, worried we would die of starvation before the Americans returned.

I grew spindly from a protracted lack of calories. I cut out pictures of prepared dishes from women's magazines, and dreamed of what they tasted like. Occasionally cases of corned beef hash came available on the black market, and dad bought up all that he could find. The Imperial Army ran short of money and printed more. Then more, and even more still. Prices soared. An egg went for 2,000 Japanese pesos.

It was commonplace to see *bayongs* full of money at the market, although food was scarce enough toward the end of the war that it didn't matter how much money one had. Japanese occupation money became worthless. People called it "Mickey Mouse" money. The value of cash became so fluid and unpredictable that people usually bartered for goods and services. Jewelry, for those who had it, also became an increasingly valuable trading commodity.

During the war our diet was bland and repetitive, consisting mostly of rice, kidney beans, cornmeal, sweet potatoes, sweet potato leaves, some varieties of fruit, and *pechay*, a spinach-like green. And we were the lucky ones. Dad had the resources to buy goods on the black market, and to insure that farmers stopped by our house when they brought their harvest to town. We also had some produce coming in from the San Francisco del Monte house.

We kept an old tom turkey, and a huge pig named Empress Josephine and one of her babies in the backyard for when we got really hungry. Mom stockpiled the canned goods in the pantry. Theft was a problem, and everything was locked up tight. When one of the servants needed something from the pantry or the china cabinet, mom pulled out a key chain the size of St. Peter's loaded with keys of every size and description.

What a treat for me when I was allowed to unlock the pantry door and pick out a can of peaches for my birthday. Mamita poured evaporated milk over the fruit. "Peaches and cream," she said, "just like in America."

Mom loved English toffees. Dad got a hold of a large tin of them from somewhere. To keep ants—a major problem in the tropics—out of the candies, mom propped the tin on top of a drinking glass in a bowl of water. This setup was kept inside a locked china cabinet. The toffees were strictly rationed: only for special occasions.

A Japanese 100-Peso note: so-called "Mickey Mouse" money

One day I heard mom gasp: "No! How could they have snuck into the cabinet?" She was referring to the ants. The first ones drowned, their bodies serving as a makeshift bridge to the water glass. The sneaky fellows even infiltrated the tightly sealed tin; inside it was crawling with ants. But it was war time, and these were no mere toffees—they were English toffees. So one by one we unwrapped the candies, brushed off the ants, and put them back in the tin.

My father was raised on bread and butter, and potatoes—not exactly staples in Manila. Dad stockpiled tins of sweet Australian butter in the pantry. Mom convinced us girls to save the butter for dad, and he learned to be frugal with its use. By the end of the war the butter had turned rancid, but dad used it anyway.

The Philippines was too humid to grow wheat. Before the war dad purchased wheat flour imported from the United States. Mom and Jimmy Ampao sifted the flour, and placed it in large cans normally used to store motor oil. The screw tops were sealed with wax. With strict rationing, the flour lasted throughout most of the war.

Toward the end, however, mom was dismayed to find insects in the flour. Jimmy Ampao never said a thing. He just sifted out the bugs and made dinner.

Troop trucks conveyed American POWs to ships in the harbor, there to be transported to Japan as slave labor. The men were thin and haggard looking, their uniforms tattered, faces burned by the sun. Whenever we saw these convoys we raised our fingers in the V-for-victory sign.

One day our *carromata* was held up behind a convoy. Mamita got so excited at the sight of Americans that she raised her hand in salute. "Vee for Veectory!" she yelled in her Spanish accent.

One of the guards ordered Irineo to stop the carriage. He held his rifle with fixed bayonet at Mamita's stomach. "You like Americans?" he yelled at her, "you march with Americans." He forced her down from the carriage and made her march with the POWs.

When the guard was distracted, Irineo spurred the horse quickly away to the home of Mamita's half-brother, Jesus Urbina. Irineo explained Mamita's plight and drove Jesus back to the docks. Jesus reasoned with the guard that Mamita was too old to be of any use building airfields. After several tense minutes she was released. From then on we more discreetly gave the victory sign to any soldiers we saw.

Twenty years later I discovered that a neighbor living

only two doors up the street had been in the Bataan Death March, and later became one of the POWs shipped to Japan from Manila Bay. Colonel John Blandy told me that during his boat ride to Japan a number of American soldiers were brought topside each day so that the Japanese could practice their bayonet technique. American officers were forced to watch, neither allowed to flinch nor to make a sound.

When bayonet practice was finished for the day, Colonel Blandy and his fellow officers hosed blood and body parts off the deck.

Not all American soldiers surrendered to the Japanese in the fall of Manila. Some fled the city with members of the Philippine Army. Reinvented as *guerrilla* fighters, they operated in the dark of night from clandestine bases, sabotaging the Japanese war effort wherever possible—blowing up train depots, troop convoys, ammunition dumps, and the like.

The Japanese high command feared the *guerrillas*, and sent special military units to outlying villages to torture the locals into revealing the location of the *guerrilla* bases. For the most part Filipinos didn't know, or didn't betray the *guerrillas*. Death was their consequence.

After the war when I was already living in Los Angeles, I discovered that an old acquaintance from Manila had been involved in clandestine activities with the *guerrillas*. Xavier "Xabi" Aboitiz and I weren't close as kids. He was three years older than me, practically a different generation from one just entering puberty. Years later, Xabi (pronounced like "Chobby") ran into mom by happenstance. That's when I learned that he had been an information runner for the *guerrillas.*

Xabi's mother, Clemencia, had been widowed at an early age. She briefly dated a man named Mr Vaughn, an executive in the Manila office of a British company. Vaughn was a dapper, portly chap with a bushy mustache. He enjoyed a lavish bachelor lifestyle replete with the finer things in life. He lived in the penthouse of the luxurious Admiralty Apartments, which had a fabulous view of the bay.

After the Japanese took the city, Vaughn passed himself off as a Spaniard to avoid internment. When the apartments in the Admiralty were confiscated for use by officers of the Imperial Air Force, Vaughn charmed the Japanese into letting him keep his place.

After Vaughn had stopped seeing Clemencia, he ran into Xabi one day on the street. Offhandedly he asked if Xabi would like to relay messages from MacArthur's command post in Australia to the *guerrillas.*

Only fifteen years old at the time, Xabi jumped at the chance, thinking it would fill his life with excitement and intrigue. It never occurred to him that it also might bring his life to a painful and precipitous end if the Japanese discovered what he was up to.

"Don't tell your mother what you're doing," Vaughn advised.

Vaughn had an interesting way of conducting his subterfuge discretely, in plain view. When there was a message for the *guerrillas*, Vaughn would flash Xabi the victory sign on the street. They met the following day at the fountain in front of Malate Church, and chatted amiably for several minutes. Vaughn handed Xabi the coded message, tipped his hat, and continued on his way. Along with the message, Xabi was given a time and location, and a code word that his *guerrilla* contact would use to identify himself.

Vaughn hid his radio antenna in the open as well. Clothes driers were a rarity in those days; laundry was hung on a line to air dry. Living on the top floor of his building as he did, Vaughn kept his clothesline on the roof. Discretely, in plain view, he wrapped his radio antenna wire around the clothesline cord.

Vaughn's operation was a simple one that ran smoothly—until the day he disappeared. One day he was part of the neighborhood, often seen about the shops and restaurants of Malate square. The next day he was gone, never to be heard from again. Xabi never learned how Vaughn had been discovered, or what became of him.

The Imperial Army Military Police were nothing if not predictable. Vaughn would have been taken where all spies were taken: to Ft Santiago, the M. P. headquarters, on the banks of the Pasig River. Once a Spanish fort, the Japanese turned Santiago into an interrogation center and torture chamber. Its very name inspired dread. One lowered one's voice when uttering it. The Military Police had their own special uniforms and weapons, and like the German Gestapo were universally feared.

After Vaughn's capture, Xabi finally understood the gravity of his situation. He suffered some sleepless nights, thinking that armed MPs were going to show up at his door and escort him off to a painful death. But apparently Mr Vaughn didn't reveal Xabi's identity.

I wondered why Mr Vaughn had risked everything to pass messages to the *guerrillas*. Xabi's answer: "Vaughn was a patriot."

My father had his own relationship with the *guerrillas*. A blonde and blue eyed Filipino, that was dad. He became a Philippine citizen in order to operate a business, but in the eyes of a world at war he was all German, a fact which placed him in considerable jeopardy, and almost constant peril.

On the one hand, he was forced to supply the Imperial Army with truck batteries and other items from his Red Star Auto Stores inventory. On the other hand, dad knew the Allies would eventually win the war, and that he risked arrest for collaborating with the enemy. So by day he cheerfully supplied batteries to the Japanese. By night he secretly donated money to the *guerrillas*.

I was kept in the dark about dad's clandestine dealings for fear I would let it slip, as children sometimes innocently do. I later learned that a sympathetic priest passed along dad's donations to the *guerrillas*. In return, dad was given so-called "emergency pesos" which were printed by the *guerrillas* and guaranteed by U. S. dollars.

Dad also demanded a written receipt, proof that he had aided the American cause. It was a dangerous undertaking for all involved. Anyone caught with emergency pesos or a donation receipt from the *guerrillas* would have met with certain death.

Even though dad was a German, and so ostensibly anti-American, the Japanese never trusted him. Red Star Auto purchased its inventory from the American company Western Auto Supply, whose logo was a red star.

The Japanese repeatedly questioned dad as to why his car batteries had the insignia of the Russian Army, which late in the war became an American ally. Dad kept telling the Japanese that the logo had no political significance, that's just how it came from the factory.

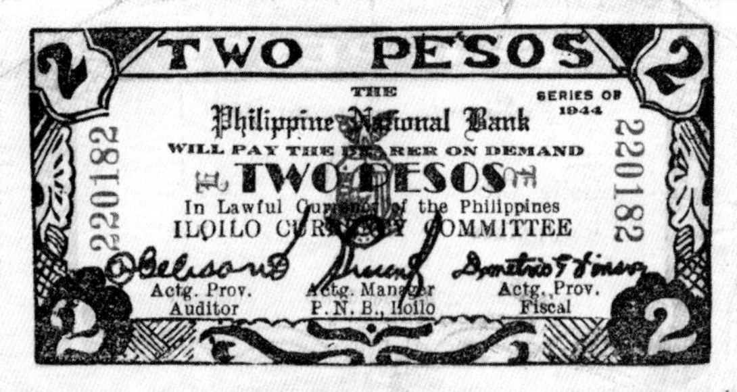

Emergency circulating note: so-called "Guerrilla Peso"

A Lieutenant Katayama of the Imperial Army was assigned to follow dad. I don't think Katayama knew exactly what he was looking for, but it was his job to catch dad at something.

The Lieutenant showed up when least expected—at dad's office, on the street, even at our house (usually at dinner time). He would pull up a chair at the dining room table and join right in. Though food was scarce we could not refuse him a meal.

I was always terrified when he was around. "Table manners" was an oxymoron to Katayama. When the meal was over he belched loudly, a compliment to the cook. But to us it seemed a vile custom.

One day the Lieutenant came into dad's office on the heels of the priest, who was delivering one of dad's receipts. Mimi Yak, dad's secretary of several years, sailed into the office, cheerfully greeted Katayama, and picked up some papers on dad's desk, including the receipt.

"I'll bring these back for your signature, Mr Berg," she said.

She smiled sweetly at Katayama, and walked out the door. Her quick thinking may have saved dad's life.

Three different times during 1943 and '44, Lt Katayama arrested dad for collaboration with the enemy. Mr Cassel called mom with the news: dad had been taken to Ft Santiago.

Each time dad was arrested, mom cried late into the night. We girls knelt beside her, praying the rosary for his safe return. We feared we would never see him again. Then at a most unexpected moment, sometimes a week or even two weeks later, dad's familiar whistle sounded outside the house and he would be home.

Dad was always released after midnight, forced to walk home alone in the dark. He never told us kids what happened to him inside the prison, but late one night I overheard muffled conversation coming from my parents bedroom.

I crept out of bed, and crouched in darkness in the hall outside their door. Dad had lifted his shirt to show mom the lash marks on his body where he had been beaten. I overheard him telling her that the prisoners slept on a bare cement floor. Mornings they were ushered out to a courtyard for a daily cold water hose bath.

Dad's cell mate was a Frenchman named LeBeque who had been working for the FBI. To maintain their sanity dad asked LeBeque to teach him French. Dad was gifted in languages. He quickly picked up the French, and was fluent in it the rest of his life.

The Japanese never got dad to confess to anything, and never could mount any evidence against him. So each time they let him go. LeBeque wasn't so lucky; he was executed.

Everyone of a certain caste in the Philippines had heard of the classical pianist Fé Mandelbaum. At fifteen she made her debut with a 60-piece Philippine Symphony Orchestra. It was only natural then, that her oldest daughter—*moi*—take up the piano. Starting at age seven, Irineo drove me to the Philippine Conservatory of Music every day after school.

My teacher was Dr Herbert Zipper, an Austrian Jew who had been interned in one of the Nazi concentration camps. Fortunately for Dr Zipper, his father had been able to obtain for him a visa to leave the country. Dr Zipper immigrated to Manila with his fiance, Trudl Dubsky, a well known ballerina whom he later married.

Mom and Dr Zipper were training me for life as a concert pianist. What an opportunity. Too bad I so quickly tired of the daily lessons. School didn't let out until 5:00 PM. With piano practice, homework, and dinner, there wasn't much time for any fun. While my friends were out playing Kick the Can in the last precious moments of sunlight, I was indoors practicing piano scales. I complained bitterly. Perhaps if I had been given some pleasant tunes to play, or songs I recognized, my life would have been different.

It took two years of persistent resistance on my part before mom buckled under the pressure of her little brat wailing that she no longer wanted to play. Finally I was allowed to quit. Pity.

As a teenager I regretted that I hadn't stuck with my lessons. At a party the most popular person was always the one at the keys. As an adult too, I would have loved to spend time playing the piano as a stress-reliever, if nothing else. Of course by then I was blaming mom for not being more forceful with me.

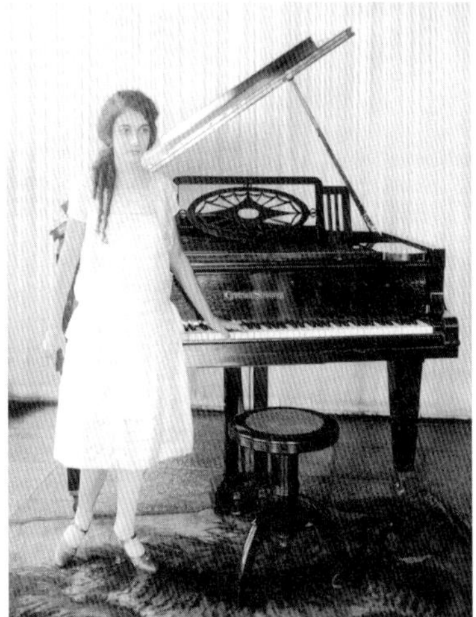

Fay at the piano, age 16

Years later, my own daughter Christine complained bitterly about tap dancing lessons. She was so persistent that I too buckled under the stress and let her quit. Then I understood: youth is served.

When war broke out in the Pacific, Dr Zipper was once again placed in a concentration camp, this time for refusing to conduct the orchestra under Japanese occupation. During his incarceration, Trudl Dubsky supported herself by teaching ballet in the rooftop garden of her apartment building.

What an opportunity for Elyse and me to learn dance from such a renowned ballerina. Her rooftop studio had a covering but no windows, so it was always delightfully cool. As there were no ballet shoes available anywhere in the city, we were forced to dance barefooted, our feet stained red by the floor tiles.

Elyse and I loved Trudl Dubsky's classes, and looked forward to the recitals we put on for the parents. Elyse was more of a tomboy. I was the prissy one. Trudl Dubsky's role selections reflected our personalities. One recital had Elyse dancing to gypsy music, complete with tambourine and a ribbon wreath in her hair. She jumped and twirled with lots of energy.

My dances were more genteel. At one recital, I carried a bar across my shoulders from which hung baskets of flowers, like a stylized version of Jimmy Ampao selling his treats. Every once in a while, I hear my "basket of flowers" melody or Elyse's gypsy dance music on the radio, but I don't know the names of the tunes, or who composed them.

It came to be known as the Great Flood of '43. It is said there are only two seasons in the Philippines—muddy and dusty. November is in the muddy season, and the typhoon that year was a doozy. Flooding was severe. The schools were closed for days. But when the waters didn't recede, the schools reopened, and Irineo ferried us to class in a *bangka*, or native canoe.

Mom and Freddie took Papito hot meals at Remedios Hospital every day. With the flooding, dad put mom on a horse and led her through the streets in chest-high water. They reminded me of a soggy version of Mary and Joseph on their journey to Bethlehem.

Elyse was born in mid-November during a fierce typhoon in which the entire city lost electricity. The hospital operated on auxiliary generators. Nine years later, while mom was planning Elyse's birthday party, another awesome storm erupted. Elyse and I stood at the window in our party dresses staring at the rising waters, heartbroken that no one could make it to the party.

I recalled some of the parties we had attended before the war. Mom had a friend, Mercedes Gonzales, who gave lavish parties for her only son, Jose Antonio. One year, Mercedes planned an American-style party—or what she thought was an American-style party—complete with barbecued food and a bale of hay. We were asked to dress in blue denim overalls; they weren't called jeans in those days.

We were notified of the party's theme months in advance so we could order the necessary items from the Sears catalog. We were so excited when the ship pulled into port with our order on board. We looked pretty cute in our blue denim duds. The party was like something out of the musical *Oklahoma*—minus the singing and dancing.

Mom eagerly awaited for her own order to arrive from the United States: a big stock of beige bouclé yarn. She had decided to make tablecloths for her daughters's hope chests. As the eldest, I was promised the first tablecloth. Mom spent endless hours crocheting hundreds of intricate little circles, then patiently stitched them together to form the most magnificent work of art. After showing it off to family and friends, she carefully wrapped it in tissue paper and stored it in her hand-carved Chinese chest.

One day I came inside to find her in tears. Someone had stolen the tablecloth. I was sad too, not so much for the loss of the tablecloth as for the love and effort that mom had put into it. Undaunted she ordered more yarn, and set to work with energy renewed. As war in the Pacific became imminent, she ordered boxes and boxes of yarn, and during the war managed to finish a tablecloth for each of her girls.

SHE SIGHED AND WHISPERED, "TOMORROW."
HOW COULD I KNOW IT WAS GOOD-BYE

4/00
X.A.

Six: Eviction

By 1944, Americans forces were retaking islands in the Pacific one by one, returning ever closer to Manila. Japanese troops patrolled the streets with a heightened sense of urgency. Food was scarce; our very lives were at risk. Yet we children were oblivious to all but our own immediate wishes and desires. We bemoaned the fact that our crayons had worn to stubs, and that our pencil boxes were old and shabby looking.

Earlier in the year, a Japanese general confiscated our house on Oregon Street. We were given twenty-four hours to vacate. Mom called the Japanese "meanies," and vowed to leave behind not one bit of furniture or stitch of draperies. To add to the insult, the Japanese commander took a liking to Patsy our pet mongoose, and forced us to leave her behind.

Dad quickly purchased a house on nearby Agno Street from a family in dire need of money. How we moved the contents of a big two-story house in a single day, without benefit of cars or trucks is a blur.

Mom enlisted the aid of our cousins, the Rodriguez boys. Along with the servants, we pushed carts on foot in sweltering heat to the new house. Our *carromata* went back and forth many times during the day loaded with goods.

We managed to move everything but one item—a massive armoire in an upstairs bedroom. It was too heavy to move down the stairs no matter what we tried. It broke mom's heart to leave it behind.

The Agno Street house became a jungle of items that had been plopped down anywhere there was a free bit of space. We worked late into the night sorting everything out. Finally we dropped from fatigue.

A butler's pantry off the dining room served as a store for dad's hoarded stock of canned goods. Fearing that poachers would try to steal the food, dad and Irineo stood armed guard at the pantry door. But out of sheer exhaustion they quickly fell asleep on the hardwood floor.

I was awakened in the predawn darkness by the sound of a man crying. I crept down the stairs and saw dad sitting at the dining room table, his head in his arms, sobbing his heart out. I stood in awe, having never seen him in such a state.

Eventually he noticed me. With sad eyes he indicated the pantry—it was empty! At midnight the room had been stacked high with canned food, sacks of rice, and sealed gallon cans of wheat flour. A few hours later the room was absolutely bare. I felt stunned and faint.

Somehow through my confusion, I heard dad say that earlier in the day someone must have seen us bringing in the food. I can only imagine how the looters were able to cart off a roomful of goods without waking up dad or Irineo.

They must have gone into the pantry many times, silently stepping over the two sleeping figures, lugging cases of canned goods, and sacks of rice and flour—all with such stealth that they weren't detected. Even the specter of dad's gun didn't deter them.

Thus began Mr Berg's private war with the neighbors.

The house was situated on a narrow side-street off of Taft Avenue, a major thoroughfare. The property was dominated by large trees and an abundance of tropical greenery. It was beautiful, but also provided plenty of potential hiding places for intruders.

Like most of the houses in the upscale sections of Manila, ours was enclosed by a stone wall that had pieces of broken glass embedded along the top. To this defense, dad added a security system of sorts: a firehouse bell mounted above the front door. A piece of rope was rigged in such a way that anyone coming through the front gate would trigger the bell.

Dad paid an exorbitant sum for a few cases of black market corned beef hash. He stacked the cases under the *capiz* shell windows along the front of the house, forming a barricade behind which he hid each night.

A few nights later, I was awakened by the ringing of the fire bell, followed by the report of dad's rifle as he fired warning shots into the yard. I imagine now, as I write this, two men facing each other in fear and darkness across a bit of ground, each wanting only to feed and protect his family. One man tries to keep what he has, the other tries to take it away. The stuff of which war is made.

Several days later, we noticed a man hobbling along the road in front of our house, his feet wrapped in bloody rags. Dad said it was probably the man who had tried to come on to our property. Perhaps he had tried to scale the wall and cut his feet on the glass, then tried the gate and tripped the bell. I felt sorry for him, but made no apology—survival was the game.

Eventually the bell stopped ringing in the middle of the night, and dad's rifle was silenced. The neighbors had gotten the message: the Berg home was impenetrable.

We settled into our new surroundings as best we could, and made friends with the neighborhood children. The Aboitiz family had two girls and two boys. The oldest boy became my longtime friend, Xabi. But back then I didn't like him at all. He was too worldly for my taste. I liked Xabi's younger brother and sister, Mike and Maria Antonia.

The Mari family had five boys. Tomas Mari, who was nicknamed Tomaset, gave me butterflies in my tummy—a bad case of puppy love. We played Spin the Bottle in a little room above the garage.

One day dad called me from the den door, telling me to bring my Betsy Wetsy doll. When I handed Betsy over to him, he closed the door in my face. After a moment of stunned silence I decided to see what he was up to. The den door had a cut glass doorknob and a huge keyhole, like the ones in old Sherlock Holmes movies. I looked through the keyhole, and saw dad remove Betsy's head. He put something inside her body cavity and replaced the head.

When he approached the door, I leaned nonchalantly against the wall, feigning boredom from the wait. Ever the actress. Dad returned my doll and went upstairs for *siesta*. When I was certain he was asleep, I took Betsy's head off. Inside was a package wrapped in tissue. Carefully I peeled back the paper. What greeted my eyes left me shocked: mom's jewelry. Some of the items were priceless family heirlooms.

Immediately I understood. The Japanese would never suspect a treasure like that being carried in a girl's doll. I vowed never to reveal the secret, and to act like what I was: a typical little girl with her doll.

By October 1944, the end was in sight. Liberation forces landed on the central Philippine island of Leyte—that was our D-Day—and by year's end would battle to the outskirts of Manila four hundred miles to the northwest. The civilian population was in desperate straits. Schools had closed indefinitely. Shops and businesses, including Berg Escolta and Red Star Auto, had run out of inventory and shuttered their windows.

Food was scarce. One by one our horses had been stolen for food (except for Pomeroy, dad's Arabian palomino, whom dad guarded like a fourth child). Trixy, our little Fox Terrier, disappeared. Dad said she ran away, but I heard him whisper to mom that some locals had stolen her for something to eat.

A young Filipino man made off with Empress Josephine's piglet. Mom chased the man down in the street. "I have three hungry girls," she pleaded, "please let me have my pig back." To her surprise, the man did give it back.

We were lucky—at least we had food to eat. Many of those less fortunate suffered horribly. We often saw starving people on the street. The incidence of beriberi was high. A wretched disease, beriberi arises from a lack of thiamine (vitamin B-1) in the diet. The heart falters. Circulation lags, causing swelling in the extremities. Sufferers have an odor about them as if they were rotting from the inside out. Eventually the untreated victim dies of heart failure.

Treatment is simple and complete: a proper diet of meat, whole grains, and green vegetables. For too many it never happened.

It was at least as bad for the animals. Our horses lived like kings compared to those used for public transportation. *Carromata* drivers packed in the people to collect more money in fares. The poor horses struggled to pull the load. The coachmen mercilessly whipped them until they had bleeding sores all over their backs.

As the war progressed and food got more and more scarce, the horses became thinner and thinner. Their mouths foamed at the bit. More than once I saw a horse collapse on the street, and prayed to God to relieve its misery.

Japanese soldiers showed up at the front door one day, and took away mom's piano. Excuse me? Mom's piano? The one her father had custom built in Vienna as a gift for her eighteenth birthday? Well, the Japs helped themselves to anything else they wanted, why not mom's piano, too? She didn't protest as she knew it would do no good.

It must have broken her heart to watch the men carting off her magnificent instrument, and with it the memories of her musical accomplishments. For years that baby grand had stood in the living room with its lid propped open as if awaiting the moment when beautiful music would emanate from its sound board. Hundreds of evenings mom had played for us after dinner, her tiny nimble fingers gliding over the ivories. In an instant it was stripped away. One suffers in many ways during a war.

One of our houseboys returned from a visit to his home town with the story of a young mother arrested by the Japanese on a fallacious charge. Produce pickers in the Philippines commonly climbed trees to gather fruit. But mango trees attracted large red fire ants which swarmed over the trunk and branches. So mangoes were harvested using a long pole with a short saw and a basket attached to one end.

The Japanese, finding the young mother guilty of whatever violation, tied her to a mango tree. Her baby was smeared with jelly and placed at her feet at the base of the tree. Ants swarmed over the baby, consuming it. The mother died her own painful death shortly thereafter.

Even now I shudder to recall the day that dad heard there was meat for sale somewhere in the city. We were all tired of a daily diet of corn bread, and the same fruits and vegetables. The prospect of meat for dinner piqued dad's taste buds, and he sent me out on horseback. Irineo saddled Patience, and down the street I rode. I have often wondered how dad could have sent me out alone like that.

I turned onto Taft Avenue and held my breath. I was alone on the street. The click of the horse's hoofs echoed on the asphalt. I had an eerie feeling of dread. I thought of turning back, but was more afraid of dad's reprimand than I was of the enemy, and so continued on.

Soon a Japanese sentry shouted at me. I had learned enough of the language to know he was telling me to stop. He grabbed the reins, and led me to a big white building with marble steps.

Apparently the soldier hadn't before encountered a young girl on horseback, and didn't know what to do with me. He ordered me to wait, and headed up the steps of the building. As he reached the door, I instinctively kicked the horse and sprinted down the street. The soldier shouted at me to stop.

I rounded the corner and disappeared from sight. The man shouted again. I put down my head and spurred Patience, riding as hard as I could. I looked back once—the soldier had rounded the corner, and was aiming his rifle at me. I heard a shot, and felt a bullet whizzing past my head.

Patience must have sensed the urgency of the situation, as she neither slowed nor faltered. Somehow we made it home. My parents came out to greet me, not realizing what had just happened.

When I got off the horse my knees were weak, and buckled under me. I crumpled in a heap on the ground, sobbing. I tried to tell my parents what had happened but couldn't get out the words. They couldn't know how close to death I had come.

Dad passed off my explanation as childish histrionics, and said he would send Elyse instead. She was feisty and daring, and would accomplish what I had failed to do. I will always be bothered by dad's apparent insensitivity.

My fear was compounded by concern for Elyse's safety. She was not yet ten years old. Barefooted and with a *bayong* full of pesos she mounted her horse, Florian. Dad gave her a paper scrawled with Japanese characters, and told her to show it to any soldier who stopped her. The characters were meaningless, but dad knew that most Japanese soldiers couldn't read, and thought the paper might fool them. Off into the asphalt battlefield rode Elyse, and returned home safely with fresh meat for dinner. I was so happy to see her.

Funny thing: after all my trauma, I don't remember dinner that night.

Seven: A Frightful End

I don't recall how we celebrated the holidays in 1942 and '43, but by late 1944, change was in the wind. Christmas trees had long since stopped arriving from Baguio. American bombers droned overhead, shelling military installations and ships in the harbor. Hunks of hot twisted metal rained down on the ground. Antiaircraft guns returned fire.

When the dust settled, we children collected the pieces of shrapnel from the field, and traded them back and forth with each other.

Dad finally decided we were really hungry. On

Christmas Eve, 1944, we ate Empress Josephine. Four days later I turned thirteen. "I am now entering my teens," I solemnly announced at my birthday dinner. My parents chuckled at my seriousness, but no doubt wondered what lay in store for me, and for us all.

American forces landed on the shores of Lingayen Gulf, fifty miles northwest of Manila, on January 8, 1945. Three weeks later they reached the outskirts of the city. Sporadic cannon fire pounded the city day and night. Bombs exploded. Tanks rumbled. Then the fires began. The retreating Japanese systematically torched the city. In every direction, as far as the eye could see, the city burned.

Example of Paper Bullets dropped from airplanes; meant to demoralize American troops.

As terrible as the Japanese occupation had been, at least it offered a predictable routine. But with an Allied invasion imminent, a still and foreboding calm settled over the city. One could feel desperation in the occupation forces. A bunker mentality settled over the city. Japanese soldiers set up gun emplacements along Taft Avenue. Traffic thinned to near nothing. People stayed indoors.

Dad let the servants go, probably because there wasn't enough food to feed them, but also to give them a chance to be with their families. Irineo and Jimmy Ampao refused to leave. They stayed with us until the day we sailed for America.

Lieutenant Katayama stopped tailing dad; there was no longer a need. The Lieutenant predicted an Allied victory, but told dad the Americans would find Manila "stone upon stone." For a long time I didn't understand his prophetic words. I'm grateful I didn't know what lay in store for us.

Pomeroy got sick—he couldn't "pass water," as dad put it—and had to be put down. With a heavy sadness, dad shot Pomeroy in the field behind our house, and left the carcass so hungry Filipinos could be put out of their misery.

American and Japanese aircraft alike dropped propaganda leaflets—so-called "paper bullets"—over the city, containing messages designed to frighten or comfort. American handbills informed us that we would soon be liberated, and promised humane treatment to any surrendering Japanese soldier.

Japanese leaflets offered rewards for information regarding American troop locations and movements. Other circulars warned civilian Filipinos that American soldiers were notorious Lotharios who would steal away their wives and daughters.

The American leaflets offered such hope to a beleaguered city. The most precious one of all contained a letter from General MacArthur which began with the words, "I have returned…," and went on to say that MacArthur had landed in Leyte, and soon would head for Manila. Our hearts raced as we read the general's message. We knelt in prayer for the brave American soldiers who would be risking their lives to liberate us.

At the internment camp at Santo Tomas, American civilian POWs received what must have been the greatest news of their lives. An American airplane flew in low over the camp, dropped an eyeglass case, and disappeared over the treetops. Inside the case was a note—"There will be a hot time on the old town tonight"—a clue that the liberating army would soon be storming the gates.

Scant days later the internees heard a rumbling in the distance and rushed to the perimeter fence. Peeking through the matting, they saw a battalion of tanks from the U. S. 1st Cavalry approaching, the Stars and Stripes emblazoned on the turrets. Sometimes the cavalry truly does come over the hill in the nick of time. What a leap of the heart those POWs must have felt. And what a hot time must have been had that night.

By early February, the American Army had battled its way south into the northern districts of Manila. In Quiapo, across the Pasig River from us, Marcelino Rodriguez prepared his family for the coming fight. Thinking they would be safest in Quiapo Church across the street from their grocery store, he moved his family there.

Many in the neighborhood had the same idea. Already the church was packed. Terrified people were praying fervently to the Black Nazareno, an icon of Christ that was prominent in the church.

My cousin Lalo, realizing that they had forgotten to bring Linda, the family dog, went looking for her. Only eighteen years old at the time, Lalo stepped outside the church. Already there was fighting in the streets nearby. The battle smoke was thick and dark in the sky, stinging Lalo's eyes. A Japanese soldier stationed at a gun emplacement outside the grocery store gave Lalo permission to go inside.

Marcelino kept a menagerie of animals on the top floor of the living quarters above the store—canaries, piglets, cats. Lalo quickly located Linda, then paused, wondering what of value he could take with him. Outside the fighting drew near. Lalo couldn't think of anything to take. Clutching Linda, he rushed back down the stairs and crossed the street to the church.

Marcelino scolded Lalo for his foolishness. The father had seen the Japanese soldier pointing his gun at Lalo's back when the boy had entered the store, deciding whether to shoot him.

The fighting swept though the neighborhood. Retreating Japanese soldiers fired machine gun rounds into the church through the stained glass windows. The people inside scattered for cover. When American soldiers later entered the church to signal the all-clear, a man climbed into the campanile and rang the bell.

People staggered out of the church as if waking from a nightmare. The destruction that greeted them was devastating. The once-quiet neighborhood lay in ruins. The grocery store was blackened and smoldering, gutted by fire. And with it their home and all of their possessions.

In a moment's time the Rodriguez family had been made refugees. They shuffled along the street with their former neighbors toward the gates on Quezon Avenue, a main thoroughfare, their belongings contained in a few pushcarts. American soldiers crawled in the ruins looking for snipers and the wounded. The burned corpses of Japanese soldiers were dropped from windows to the street below. Many of the recently displaced spat on the charred remains as they passed.

A few miles away, we had no knowledge of the Rodriguez family's fate. The American advance pushed the Imperial Army across the Pasig River, and south and west toward the bay. A wave of displaced people washed over us. All day and much of the night refugees came by the house looking for temporary shelter and something to drink, a bit of food if we could spare it. They told us horror stories of Japanese atrocities. Entire families of our friends had been wiped out.

My other cousins, the Rocha family, lived south of us in the Malate district. When the Battle for Manila commenced, their number, some two dozen strong, gathered in the home of Tony Rocha Sr, and his wife Josefina. Their daughter Lita and I had been enrolled together at the American School until my transfer to Assumption Convent.

In a scene being replayed throughout the city with monotonous regularity, the Rochas saw the houses on their street burned, and innocent neighbors slaughtered trying to flee. When their own house was torched, the Rocha family managed to escape unharmed, and later took shelter under a stone staircase in the charred remains of the house next door.

The next day Josefina rummaged in the debris to salvage what she could of their possessions, but all was lost. Tony gathered corrugated roofing material to construct a shelter. Without warning the fighting started again. They dashed across the yard to retake their position under the stairs.

Out of the anarchy of noise and smoke, a servant's voice beckoned them from the garage at the back of the property. In a fateful moment husband and wife parted. Tony continued on. Josefina heeded the servant's call and took shelter in the garage.

When the shelling stopped, an agonizing cry could be heard from the back of the property. Thinking someone mortally wounded, Tony went to investigate. He found the servant hunched over Josefina's lifeless body, wailing in anguish. Tony dug a grave in the yard. He and the children laid her to rest.

Fighting in the area was intense. Machine gun fire and mortar rounds exploded all around them. Devastated, the Rocha family gathered under the stairs with some of the neighbors to consider their next move. Someone had heard a rumor that the internment camp at Santo Tomas University had been liberated.

Some of the Rocha clan thought it prudent to make their way toward American held territory. Others argued that, even though not of German decent, they would be safer at the German Club, thinking it immune to Japanese attack. Neither faction could persuade the other. Eventually the Rochas split up, agreeing to reunite later.

Eleven family members went off in the direction of the German Club. Tony and the others set off for the university. One of their number had a huge pig like our Empress Jo. Fearing they would be gunned down crossing the street, they sent the pig wandering out ahead of them to see if it would draw fire.

Sometimes out of nerves or perhaps for cruel sport Japanese soldiers shot at the pig. Though wounded, the pig was so fat that the bullets didn't kill it. When the pig was shot, the group laid in hiding until the threat had passed. Otherwise they figured it was safe to cross. In like fashion they made their way up first one street, then another.

Fighting was heavy, the going slow. By nightfall they had traveled only a short distance. They spent that first night in the ruins of a burned-out house. They laid awake in the dark, listening to the gunfire and fretting their fate. The next day, exhausted but alive, they pressed on toward the university. Street by street they made their way. As it had the previous day, the huge pig preceded them, bloody but unbowed.

Later that morning they encountered a unit of Japanese soldiers picking its way from cover to cover up the street toward them. The Rochas cowered behind some rubble. The soldiers passed perilously close to them. They noticed the civilians, but were too preoccupied with American soldiers to bother shooting civilians. The group breathed in relief when the squad had passed.

Then a Japanese soldier peeled off his unit and came back toward them with rifle in hand. My cousin Lita thought that was it—they were all going to be slaughtered where they lay cowering like wounded animals. But instead the soldier knelt down on one knee, and tied his boot.

Glancing over his shoulder to make sure he wasn't

being observed, he leaned in close to them and pulled something out of his shirt to show them: a crucifix on a chain. "Me Christian," he murmured. "Tomorrow boom-boom." He gave them a meaningful look and ran to catch up with his unit.

The group took advantage of the warning by taking shelter. Across the street was a thick stone wall. Beyond it lay an empty field similar to ours on Agno Street. They sent the pig out ahead of them, and when it was safe hurried across the street in small groups.

A young neighbor family with two small children was caught in some crossfire; the mother was struck in the arm. Father and children made it safely to the other side before realizing that the mother was down. Tony had to restrain the kids from running to her side.

During a lull in the fighting, Tony and the woman's husband carried her off the street. She was bleeding profusely from a wound in her arm. A Dr Lopez came forward to examine the wound, and determined that the arm would have to be amputated if the woman would survive. She choked down some liquor as her only anesthetic.

Quickly the arm was excised. She survived the surgery, but later suffered a trauma-induced heart attack and couldn't be revived. For the second time in as many days, Tony Rocha buried a woman in front of her children. Her grave was shallow—every minute spent out in the open was perilous.

They noticed a row of bullet holes chipped into the wall about four feet off the ground, evidence of the Japanese practice of lining up victims against a wall and

Many of those in the field were wary of the scout's motives, wondering if he secretly was working for the Japanese. Somehow the scout convinced them his offer was genuine.

The group gathered itself, preparing to leave. A woman produced a crucifix. Everyone kissed it and prayed for guidance. The scout went first, picking his way carefully through the minefield. Then went the pig—still alive—just in case. The fighting had passed. They made it safely to Santo Tomas, which indeed had been liberated.

LA VERDAD NO ES UNA AMENAZA

Eight: Days of Hell, Nights of Hell

overleaf—title reads: "The truth is not a threat"

Refugees passed daily through the field behind our house. With frightening regularity we were told the same stories of Japanese atrocities against civilians. Dad quickly heard enough, and accelerated his plans for our safety. Irineo and Jimmy Ampao helped him break a hole through the stone wall in the backyard to the empty field beyond. They worked at night to avoid detection, and camouflaged the opening with leaves and branches.

Dad took charge of people moving into the field, offering advice and consolation, and teaching them how to prepare for the coming battle for Manila.

We filled steamer trunks with clothing, towels, and linens to absorb bullets and flying shrapnel. The trunks were stacked and arranged in the shape of a horseshoe. The lot was covered with thick Oriental rugs.

We girls were instructed to fill a *bayong* with a change of clothing, food for two days, and whatever prized possessions would fit. Into my bag went my favorite Hardy Boys mystery story and my First Communion prayer book. On top went the extremely valuable Betsy Wetsy doll, along with some of Betsy's clothes that Mamita had made.

"One night I will come to your rooms and awaken you," dad said. "Without a word, grab your *bayongs* and follow me."

We were drilled in silently descending the stairs in the dark, climbing through the hole in the wall, and scrambling into our shelters. As it happened, the field became our salvation. Had the Japanese not kicked us out of our house on Oregon Street, we would have had no escape route out the back of the house, and quite likely would not have survived the machine gunners waiting in the front yard when our house was torched.

The older I get, the more I realize how chance occurrences—seemingly insignificant events at the time—can have a profound effect for good or ill in one's life.

After lunch one day, dad went upstairs for *siesta*. I was playing a game on the living room floor with Tomaset, and Xabi and Mike Aboitiz. As usual, there was fighting in the distance, an everyday occurrence. But once we had figured out that the danger was elsewhere, we went on with our lives.

Suddenly the pitch of the gunfire intensified. It sounded as if it was coming from Taft Avenue. Irineo raced into the house. "Mr Berg! Mr Berg!" he shouted excitedly, "Mrs Berg has been wounded." Dad dashed down the stairs and followed Irineo outside.

An explosion rocked the house. Tomaset pulled me down behind the sofa. He grabbed some throw pillows to cover our heads. Suddenly it seemed as if the entire war was being waged in our front yard. Between explosions, Tomaset pulled me out from behind the sofa, and led me toward the back of the house. A mighty concussion disturbed our balance—*whoosh!* A heavy sliding mahogany door blasted off its tracks, luckily blowing away from us.

We raced into the yard and ducked through the hole in the garden wall. The field beyond was littered with debris, the air filled with smoke. People were crying and screaming. Desperately I searched for my family. Tomaset yelled something unintelligible at me, and pulled me under the thick Oriental rugs.

It was difficult to breathe through the dust and smoke. We mumbled the rosary. I was shaking uncontrollably. Tomaset put his arms around me. I told him I loved him. He said he loved me too.

When the bombing stopped we crawled out. Bomb fragments littered the ground around us. The stack of rugs under which we had lain was so thick that flying shrapnel literally had bounced off of it. I silently thanked God for our lives. After a hurried good-bye, Tomaset set off in search of his family.

Luckily none of my family were killed. But several

were injured. Shrapnel was embedded in mom's ankle. Nearby, Mamita lay moaning. A shard of metal had ripped out a chunk of her thigh. Elyse had a bullet wound in her leg. Luckily, the shot had passed through without striking artery or bone. Again, the hand of God protecting us.

When we had collected ourselves, dad ushered us inside the house. The living room was a shambles. The floor and stairs were strewn with boards, plaster, and smoldering embers. Had Tomaset and I stayed crouched behind the sofa we might not have survived.

Dad carried me up to the second floor. A shell had sheared off a corner of the house. Part of the wall had blown away. The room was open to the sky. Dad's mattress was riddled with shrapnel holes.

Dad recalled that Irineo had awakened him from his nap when mom was wounded. "I wouldn't have survived," dad said, "if your mother hadn't been hurt."

He placed a bomb frag in my hand and closed my fingers around it. With tears in his eyes he said, "Pray to God your children never experience what you have today."

Little did we know that the worst was yet to come.

Battles raged around us. At any time of the day or night we dived for cover when the shelling commenced. With the upper floor partially destroyed, mattresses were brought downstairs and set up on the enclosed porch at the back of the house. Nights we lay in the sultry darkness, listening to the fighting all around us. The sky glowed with an eerie red light. During the day, refugees passed through the yard, recounting their tales of horror. Through it all we kids managed to play with our friends.

One afternoon a squad of Japanese soldiers came into the compound. Everything stopped in the yard. Immediately I thought: *we're all going to die now.*

The soldiers wore cloth caps with flaps in back that shielded their necks from the tropical sun. Swords dangled from their belts. They motioned the women into a circle. Men and children were dismissed. Though barely thirteen, I was ordered to remain. The soldiers talked animatedly amongst themselves. I didn't fully understand until years later what was happening: *We were going to be raped!*

It took a while for the soldiers to sort out their preferences. They argued back and forth. Irineo ran to get dad in the front part of the house. Dad came out and saw the women standing silently with their heads bowed. Immediately he knew what was happening. He had picked up enough Japanese to be able to communicate, and greeted the officer in charge. Even playing the humble supplicant dad commanded their attention, and coaxed the men indoors.

A while later they came back out, smiling and laughing. They shook hands with dad and left as quickly as they had come. Inside, dad had told the soldiers that none of them—soldiers and civilians alike—would survive the battle for Manila. And since death was imminent, they might as well break out the case of Irish whiskey that he had hidden under his bed. Dad got them snockered, and that was the end of it.

Until later that night. I was sound asleep on the patio. Dad nudged me awake. He gave me a pack of Japanese cigarettes and a bowl of rice. I looked at him questioningly: what was this?

He stroked my hair, and whispered that one of the soldiers had come back later in the afternoon. The soldier told dad in heavily accented English that he had a "rovery" daughter, and wanted to give her—me—his daily ration. I was disgusted by the gesture without fully understanding why, and burst into tears. Dad held me tightly for what seemed a long time.

The fires in the city burned closer and closer in an ever widening arc. Every face that found its way into our field had a haunted, empty look. A few talked about the horrors they had witnessed. All were grateful to be alive.

Papito was released from Remedios Hospital. He and Mamita locked up their house, and moved in with us. It was a happy occasion in an otherwise bleak situation. We started sleeping with our clothes on. Soon after that, dad gently shook us awake.

"It's time," I heard him say in the darkness.

It was quiet outside; I don't know how he knew the end was near. As we had playacted many times, we got out of bed and grabbed our *bayongs.* Silently we descended the stairs, tiptoed into the backyard, and crawled through the hole in the wall.

No sooner had we reached the empty field than the

nighttime calm was shattered. Machine gun fire opened up on Taft. People ran by on the street beyond the wall, shouting in fear and confusion. All was chaos. I heard the sound of wooden sticks clattering together at the front of the house. I couldn't imagine what it was.

Soon to my dismay I discovered that the Japanese were piling whatever kindling they could find—wooden Venetian blinds in our case—in front of houses up and down the street. The stacks were doused with gasoline and set on fire. Lieutenant Katayama's prediction that Manila would be left "stone upon stone" echoed in my head.

Methodically the Japanese mowed down people as they ran screaming from their houses. From the shelter in the field, I watched the back of our house explode in a ball of fire. Flames spread to the second floor. My bedroom lit up, devouring my treasures. I remember thinking: *There goes my bed... There go my books and my dolls...*

I didn't cry. No one did. We huddled, speechless, numb, each lost in his own thoughts. I still can hear the fire raging, still can see it leap from the windows in tongues of red and yellow, flaming material crashing to the ground below in a hail of embers.

The heat was so intense that dad formed a bucket brigade to wet down our shelters. The water table is close to ground level in Manila, and dad had only to dig down a few inches to find water. He scooped up bucketsful, passing it down a line to Papito, mom, Irineo, and Jimmy Ampao. The water evaporated in a cloud of steam upon hitting the rugs.

As quickly as the battle had started it was over. The Japanese completed their gruesome task and moved on to another block. After all of the deafening noise, an eerie silence settled over the compound.

I don't remember sleeping that night, nor where I would have curled up had I wanted to. The shelter was sopping wet, uninhabitable. My *bayong* was soaked with water. The Hardy Boys book was a swollen mess. The red dye of Betsy's dress bled on everything. But inside her belly, the jewels were safe.

The next day we emerged from the field to assess the damage. The neighborhood lay in ruins. Mom and I sifted through the remains of what once had been our home. A little neighborhood boy lay alone on the ground near the front of our house. There was a bullet hole in his chest, but not a trace of blood. He looked asleep.

Numb with grief, mom and I toed the debris, crying silently. We didn't say anything beyond an occasional cry of regret. We mourned the loss of family photographs, and of mom's recipe collection. Mom found a melted portion of a silver water pitcher that had been one of her own wedding presents.

My heart keened when I remembered the tablecloths that she had painstakingly crocheted for our eventual marriages, now ashes. It was all so sad, yet a small price to pay for survival.

We settled into life in the field, waiting by day, sleeping fitfully at night. Potable water was a problem, the threat of typhus and other diseases ever present. Mom scooped water out of a hole dug in the ground. Jimmy

Ampao boiled it over a wood fire. We waited for the mud to settle in the glass before drinking.

Fortunately none of us got sick. Mom gave a prayer of thanks. Had it been peacetime, she said, we probably all would have gotten sick. To this day I consider it a miracle—to drink tainted water and live to tell about it.

Advancing American tanks rumbled nearby. Japanese soldiers returned fire from their battlements. With his blonde hair and blue eyes, dad really stood out in a crowd. Most of the time he wore sleeveless white undershirts so as not to be mistaken for an American soldier and shot on sight.

We hung wine bottle corks like jewelry from strings around our necks. Dad drilled us in holding the cork between our teeth, covering our eyes with our fingers, and plugging our ears with our thumbs. He explained that covering the eyes would prevent them from popping out from the concussion of an exploding shell. Our thumbs would protect our eardrums. The cork would keep our mouths open to let air circulate through our bodies, helping avert internal damage.

Whenever shelling started from ships in the harbor, we popped our corks in our mouths and ducked into the shelter. After one such attack we heard a Filipino man moaning across the field. He was sitting on open ground with his back against a tree, his legs splayed. Periodically he cried out for his mother. It was unnerving.

When the fighting flared, this man took the brunt of the attack in the form of bullets and flying shrapnel. Each time I looked at him he had fresh wounds. Finally, dad told mom to give him an overdose of morphine. All we had in our first aid kit was a four-year-old vial. Mom administered the narcotic. Mercifully the man's crying stopped. We thought he had died, but a few hours later he started moaning again. Apparently the morphine had lost its potency. It took him a long time to die.

A portion of thick cement wall that had been part of our house remained standing. Dad reasoned that the wall would provide added protection, and decided to move our shelter. Mom argued that we had put so much effort into the shelter we had, why start over?

Dad was insistent, as only he could be, and the process began. After the move was completed, our freestanding shelter was then backed by a thick wall. There was an opening in front for access, and our precious rugs on top.

A lot of time and energy went into this effort. By nightfall we fell asleep totally exhausted. The next morning we slowly emerged like moles squinting up at the sun. Dad already was up. He was looking at the spot where the shelter previously had been.

Another family had taken over that site. A direct hit in the night had killed them all. A look of horrified realization flickered in mom's eyes. Dad never said a word.

Mom always said that February 13, 1945 was the worst night of our lives. That morning we had found an unexploded mortar shell at the entrance to our shelter: a dud. Irineo placed the cast iron sink from our burned-out kitchen over the shell so that no one would accidentally kick it and perhaps set it off. Mom might have seen this as a good omen, but she had such a fear of the unknown that she wasn't at all certain that we would be okay.

That night the fighting resumed. It was worse than anything we had previously experienced, an almost continuous barrage of explosions, blinding flashes of light, noise and dust throughout the night. We lay huddled in our shelter, deathly afraid, praying the terror would end. It was difficult to breath and to see. We had to shout in each other's ears to be heard.

Dad gave each of us girls some peach brandy to calm us. It was smooth going down. I liked it. He nudged the bottle against my arm tempting me to take more, and then more. I got dizzy, a feeling I didn't much like. The shelter was spinning, the sound of exploding shells altogether different than what I was used to.

Dad coaxed me to lie down beside Elaine, and stretched out over both of us. Mom laid on top of Elyse. I asked him what he was doing.

"I can't protect you from a direct hit," he said between mortar rounds, "but I can shield you from flying shrapnel."

Fearing for his safety, I protested. He shushed me and told me not to worry. He had lived his life, he said, and wanted his daughters to have a chance to live theirs. Finally, despite the fierceness of the fighting, the alcohol put me to sleep.

The following morning it was ominously quiet, the silence unnerving after the tumult of the night before.

The smell of spent explosives hung heavily in the air. We emerged from our shelters not knowing what to expect.

Our entire extended family was alive and intact. The Aboitiz family also had survived the night. The Mari family, however, suffered a grievous loss. Tomas, the elder Mari, had been mortally wounded, and clung tentatively to life.

A large frag had sliced open his midsection. He was holding his side to prevent his intestines from spilling out on the ground. Knowing his father was near death, the oldest son, Pocholo, began digging a grave.

A stranger appeared at our gate, a Filipino man saying that the Americans had advanced as far as Taft Avenue, and were expected to pass through our area. As had the Rochas, we looked at this man with skepticism. Perhaps he had been planted by the Japanese.

Xabi vouched for him, recognizing him as a houseboy from the neighborhood. We thanked the man and prepared ourselves for the coming fight.

A while later, Irineo approached dad to say that some Americans were in the street outside the field. Dad asked for a description of the soldiers, wanting to make sure they were really Americans and not Koreans fighting in the Japanese army. Korean soldiers were typically larger than their Japanese counterparts, and wore green uniforms. Irineo said the soldiers weren't blonde and blue-eyed like he thought all Americans were. They spoke a funny kind of English, too, but he was positive they were Americans.

Wanting to see for himself, dad followed Irineo across the field. Near the entrance they crawled on their bellies for fear of a sniper's bullet. At the gate dad discovered the soldiers really were Americans, a unit of the 1st Cavalry. Many were dark skinned, of Hispanic decent, further tanned from their time in the tropics. The "funny accent" was because most of the men were from Texas. The houseboy's warning had been correct: the Japanese retreat was headed our way; a fearsome battle was expected.

A feeling of hope mixed with panic surged through the compound. Xabi told Pocholo that there was no time to finish his father's grave. Pocholo would have to leave his father behind, alive, though barely. Mom pulled one of her hand-embroidered Chinese tablecloths from a steamer trunk. Dad covered Tomas Mari with the cloth, a final gesture of decency for a dying man.

We gathered our *bayongs* and filed off the field, the horrors of the last several days etched on our faces. Jimmy Ampao carried his cooking pot with the remains of the cooked rooster in it. Mrs Lulu Mari looked like a zombie. She had herself been wounded, and was reluctant to leave her dying husband's side. Her sons forced her into a push cart and wheeled her out. A widow at an early age, and now with four boys to care for alone.

At the gate Tomaset turned to find me. Our eyes met across the field. Then he was gone. Some of the people leaving the field tossed their "Mickey Mouse" occupation money in the air. The bills fluttered to earth like confetti, worthless trash that no one bothered to gather.

Nine: The City After

overleaf: the Botanical Gardens destroyed, Manila, 1945

When we emerged from the field, we gasped at the destruction that greeted us. Manila had been a magnificent city, the "pearl of the Orient." Now it was totally demolished, an arid wasteland. Rubble in every direction as far as the eye could see.

The charred husks of a few buildings remained standing, but were gutted and riddled with bullet and shrapnel holes. The smell of death hung heavily in the air. And bodies, everywhere, hundreds of them, bloated and covered with flies.

American soldiers were everywhere. Military jeeps and trucks motored back and forth. We had prayed for liberation for so long and so passionately, but were too mentally and physically exhausted to work up a lot of enthusiasm.

Our field had been a refuge for displaced persons hoping to survive. Now we Bergs were displaced. We were a sorry lot—dirty, hungry, exhausted, disheveled. And injured. Elyse's bullet wound had become badly infected. Dad carried her on his shoulders. Mamita's thigh wound made walking difficult and painful, even with Papito's help. Mom limped along on her infected ankle, supported by Irineo.

We plodded without direction, not knowing where we were going or what we would do when we got there. Eventually we came to a grassy spot and sat down to rest. The grass felt cool after the dust and debris of the field.

Jimmy Ampao distributed the remainder of the rooster from his cooking pot, handing each of us a piece. I gratefully accepted the drumstick, but it was so tough that I couldn't tear the meat from the bone. I cried in frustration borne of hunger. Wiping my tears, I noticed a small circle of Filipino boys, half naked, looking at us as if we were the luckiest people on earth. One of the boys was looking at me, crying. I offered him my drumstick, and he ran off with it.

That scene has stayed with me through the years. I had food, and cried because I couldn't eat it. The little boy cried because he didn't even have that.

Dad decided that our house on Oregon Street must still be standing. The Imperial Army had confiscated it for use as a command post. Dad reasoned that they wouldn't bomb their own headquarters. We gathered our meager belongings and trudged off in that direction. Passing a church, we noticed a lone soldier cleaning his rifle on the steps. Dad said to me, "Today is Valentine's Day, Evie. Give that soldier a hug. Thank him for liberating us."

I crept up on the soldier from behind and threw my arms around his neck. He jumped from nerves, momentarily clutching his rifle. After all he must have been through in the previous months, it's a wonder he didn't try to shoot me first, and ask questions later. When he recovered from the shock he seemed grateful for my thanks and waved to my family.

After what seemed a long walk, we stopped at a little *nipa* hut. The hut was half burned out, surrounded by debris. We ate GI rations, and stretched out on the bare wood floor. My *bayong* served as a pillow. Dad told us to be especially quiet during the night as there might still be Japanese snipers about.

Dad and Jimmy Ampao took turns standing guard. Despite being awakened throughout the night by sporadic gunfire, I had the most amazing feeling of peace, and slept well for the first time since the onset of war.

The following morning we continued on to Oregon Street. The streets were littered with rubble. The going was slow. I mis-stepped over a sheet of iron roofing material, and sliced my leg rather deeply.

Mom was worried about her brother Freddie and his family. Had they survived? Where were they? Fortunately we encountered friends who had recently spoken to them: they were alive and well. Freddie had expressed concern for us, we learned, but would have to wait for news of our situation.

Only one block of houses remained intact in the entire city of Manila. Our house was one of them. It had been a bitter moment indeed when the Japanese evicted us. But that event also saved our house from destruction. What a glorious sight to see it standing there—1640 Oregon Street. One can't appreciate something quite as deeply until it is lost.

An American soldier was standing guard at the front gate. Dad introduced himself as the owner of the house. The soldier laughed. He said at least two hundred people had made the same claim already that day, and it was early yet. Dad would have to prove that the house was his. But how? Government buildings had all been destroyed, and with them the property records.

Dad asked to speak to the man in charge, and there was a brief exchange. In the end we were allowed to move in, on condition that the Captain's men be given the freedom to use the house. Dad immediately agreed. How could he not? The men had been fighting in the jungles, some of them for years. Who more deserved to take their meals indoors, to have a roof to shield their heads from the hot sun, or to enjoy an occasional bath?

The child in the midst of battle was now in the company of handsome American soldiers, and not near old enough to wear lipstick or even a bra. The soldiers were kind to us. They shared their rations with us: candy bars, C-rations, Spam, hard cookies, cans of sardines. We never went hungry again. When the soldiers noticed wounded among us, they referred us to a local army hospital.

Some hospital: a tent with a red cross stitched on the side. The doctor said he couldn't treat us; wounded American soldiers took priority. Dad pleaded our case. He was given some packets of a new miracle drug called sulfa, which had been developed during the war to fight infection. But still the doctor wouldn't look at our wounds.

Well my father, the German pit bull, planted his feet and crossed his arms. He argued that American ordnance had wounded his family, and by God American medicine would treat it. He fixed the doctor with his best withering stare, the heat of which could be intense, let me tell you. Finally the doctor relented.

Mom and Mamita's wounds were relatively minor. So was mine. Eventually the wound healed, though an ugly scar serves as a daily reminder. Elyse's wound was quite a bit more serious—her leg was badly infected. The doctor did what he could for her, then pulled my parents aside and told them to pray.

I cried when I later overheard dad telling mom that the leg might have to be amputated. Elyse was such a wonderful dancer; better than I ever hoped to be. The thought that she might lose a leg was a bitter one.

After months in the jungle, the GIs loved being in our house, and especially taking a hot bath in our big tub. The majority of them were from the 1st Cavalry. Some of the men ruffled my hair, and said, "Hey, you look like Dorothy Lamour. Look me up when you're sixteen." I was a far cry from her—the only resemblance being my dark eyes—but if fighting in the jungles had blurred their vision, then so be it.

I vividly remember the flies. Oh, my gosh! Many dead bodies all over the city remained to be buried. The resulting fly infestation was so horrific that we ate with one hand covering our plates, and shooed the flies away between bites.

I couldn't find Patsy our pet mongoose anywhere, and asked a soldier if he had seen her. He told me a sad story. Apparently Patsy had playfully jumped on the shoulders of one of the men, scaring him half to death. Reflexively the man had shot her, his nerves frayed from months in the jungle. I recalled surprising the soldier on the church steps the day before, suddenly grateful that he had been cleaning his rifle at the time.

My neighbor, Esperanza "Espie" Briones, was envious of all the attention we were getting. The Briones family had also returned to their home, but her father was a senator so they didn't have to share their house with GIs.

Espie spent the better part of each day with us. She and I developed a crush on a soldier from Wisconsin named Virgil Odum. He was so cute, with blond hair and blue eyes. He told me to look him up when I got older. I bet he said that to all the girls. I later tried to locate Virgil through various civilian and military organizations, but to no avail. I hope he survived the fighting in Okinawa.

One of the soldiers we grew especially close to was Joe Barragan from Albuquerque, New Mexico. Joe always had extra candy bars, and kept us laughing. Mom called him *barrigon*, which in Spanish means "one with a big tummy."

My father, ever the entrepreneur, set up a milkshake stand in the ruins of Berg Escolta. He fashioned a lean-to out of sheets of rummaged iron, bought powdered milk from the U. S. Army, and made ice with portable generators. So many were bemoaning the fact that they had lost everything, but dad rolled up his sleeves and went to work. He thought it wise that the family stick close to home, so I never saw this ice cream parlor of his. But he came home at the end of the day with stories of all the people who lined up for one of his shakes. The GIs especially loved them as reminders of home.

One day the house was bustling with soldiers. The next day they shipped out. It was sad to see them go. We later learned they were fighting in Okinawa, a first step toward invading Japan. The fighting was intense on Okinawa; some of my new American friends probably didn't make it home.

The first night alone in our old house was one of the most terrifying nights I experienced during or after the war. Our extended family—mom and dad, Elyse, Elaine, and I, Mamita and Papito, and Irineo and Jimmy Ampao—congregated in the master bedroom.

There were plenty of rooms to sleep in, but we stayed together. Perhaps fear joined us, or simply that we had gotten used to living together in close quarters. We curled up on the bare wood floors, and settled in for the night.

The armoire that had been too heavy to move to Agno Street was still there. As an added precaution, dad and the men heaved it against the door.

That afternoon some soldiers had told us that snipers were still about, and that their "mopping up" operation would last for several more days. Dad warned us that if we heard any noise during the night we were to remain perfectly quiet. We laid in the dark and listened to the intermittent gunfire filtering up from the street below. I was exhausted from our travails, and quickly fell asleep.

Sometime after midnight I was suddenly awakened. It was quiet. I listened intently in the darkness, wondering what had aroused me. Then I heard it: the sound of a footfall somewhere in the house. I felt my father tense beside me; he had heard it too. Another footfall, the steps slow and clumsy, and the sound of metal scraping wood. Whoever it was, was climbing the stairs, dragging something metallic behind him.

We were all awake by then, alert with fear. None of us dared make a sound, even little Elaine. Up the stairs the boots came, heavy and slow: *clomp... clomp... clomp...* The man—I assumed it was a man—reached the top of the stairs and entered the room adjacent to us. He seemed in no hurry, and made no attempt to hide his presence.

He rummaged around in the room for a time, then returned to the hallway. Slowly he approached the room we were in, his metallic object scraping along the floor. I was so frightened I could hardly breathe.

The doorknob rattled, and banged against the armoire. The man pushed on the door, but to no avail. He couldn't budge the armoire. Eventually he gave up and clomped down the hall to the next room. As he had before, he rummaged around as if looking for something. After an eternity, he stomped down the hall past our door, kicking it in frustration. Noisily he descended the stairs, dragging the metal behind him. Finally there was silence again.

The next thing I remember is awaking to a blinding sun beating in the window, and the sound of voices downstairs. There was a trail of blood in the hall, and on the stairs. As I often did, I slid down the banister. Already my panic of the night before had waned.

Dad told me the noise we heard was a Japanese officer looking for a place to die. The metallic sound had been his sword cracking on the steps as he climbed, and dragging on the floor. He had succumbed at the foot of the stairs in a pool of his own blood. Already dad had buried him in the front yard. He took me out on the porch, and indicated a freshly spaded mound of dirt at the foot of a rubber tree.

Ours was not the only house in the family to survive the war intact. Aunt Carmen's house also had been spared. In a neighborhood leveled by Japanese fire bombs, theirs was the only structure left standing amidst the rubble, aided by a ghost from the past.

When Aunt Carmen was little, the Rickards family chauffeur was a Japanese man named Kawano. Carmen remembered him driving her to grammar school. Eventually Kawano returned to Japan and fell out of touch. Many years later, toward the end of the war,

Carmen and Freddie and their baby daughter Carmencita were living with Carmen's parents.

One day a phalanx of soldiers approached the house led by a colonel in full regalia. The sight of the Imperial Army descending on the Rickards house sent a panic through the neighborhood: everyone assumed that Freddie had been mistaken for an American because of his blue eyes, and would be arrested.

With trepidation, Mr Rickards invited the soldiers inside. The colonel looked around slowly, his eyes coming to rest on Carmen.

"Hello, Nena," he said, using her childhood nickname. "Remember me? I'm Kawano."

What a shock that encounter must have been for the Rickardses. There was a hurried, nervous reunion with their old employee. Kawano had steadily risen in rank over the years, and was then in charge of a nearby barracks.

The colonel had chosen that particular day to visit the Rickards family: he wanted to spare their lives. Though not generally known, the internment camp at Santo Tomas University had recently been liberated. The Imperial Army was about to retreat, and level the city in its wake. Kawano told the Rickardses to stay on the south side of the house, as the shelling would come from the north.

Later that afternoon, Mr Rickards ushered his family into a shelter beneath the house. Two of Carmen's brothers, Walter and Ralph (aka "Chiqui"), didn't trust Kawano's motives. In defiance, or perhaps only to smoke, they went to the north part of the house and lit cigarettes to calm their nerves. Mr Rickards thought his sons were too young to smoke, and wouldn't tolerate it in his presence.

The fighting began. A shell hit the north side of the house as Kawano had predicted. Walter was mortally wounded. Chiqui eased him into the shelter through a crawl space in the floor. As he grabbed Walter's arms to lower him down, he felt mostly shattered bone and bloody pulp. Inside the shelter, Walter told Chiqui, "I'll probably lose my arm. Take my guitar, I won't need it." He asked his father if he could smoke, a request that was not denied.

Ironically the oldest Rickards brother, Robert "Bertie," a young doctor, was on his way home at that moment. He had gone to visit his fiancee, Conchita Sotelo. Her father had suffered a heart attack and required medical attention. When the fighting erupted Bertie tried to get home, but a Japanese sentry turned him back.

At a break in the fighting Chiqui and his father pulled Walter out of the shelter, and carried him on an improvised litter to a Dr Goitia's house several blocks away. The doctor's mother and pregnant wife both had recently been murdered by the Japanese. The doctor was so devastated by his loss that he was unable to care for Walter, but told Rickards to help himself to whatever medical instruments were in the examining room.

Mr Rickards and Chiqui carried Walter to the medical office at the back of the house and placed him on a table. Without benefit of anesthesia nor any medical experience, Mr Rickards cut Walter's arm off, desperately hoping that this would stop the bleeding and save his life. Later, not knowing what else to do for Walter, they carried him home again.

That night, soldiers swept through the neighborhood torching houses with Molotov cocktails. As had happened elsewhere, cocked machine guns were waiting for people as they ran from their homes. Colonel Kawano gave strict instructions to spare the Rickards home. Thus the family survived. All except Walter. He lay dead in the living room with some candles around him.

After the Japanese were ousted, Mr Rickards told the Americans what had happened. Some soldiers wrapped Walter in an American flag and buried him in the yard under his parents's bedroom window.

Eventually Bertie found his way home. Conchita's house had been destroyed, and Bertie brought her along to live with them. Even in wartime, the bounds of propriety required their marriage if they would live together under one roof. A priest performed a hasty ceremony in the ruins of the local church. Bertie wore his father's wedding ring, Conchita wore his mother's.

Doubt persisted in Bertie's mind: if he had been home, perhaps he could have saved Walter's life. A year later he exhumed Walter's body. An autopsy revealed signs of internal bleeding. There was nothing Bertie could have done, the knowledge of which brought a measure of peace to the Rickards family.

MI FILIPINAS QUERIDA
11/97 X.A.

Ten: Renewal

overleaf—caption reads: "My precious Philippines"

Japan surrendered the Philippines in the spring of 1945. A sense of peace returned to Manila. My parents went to salvage what they could from our shelter in the field behind the Agno Street house. Mom was heartbroken to discover her treasures missing, pilfered by looters. Dad salvaged some of the paper bullets the Americans had dropped, and some of the Japanese "Mickey Mouse" script, which was worthless save for historical interest.

I felt bad for Papito. He had spent most of his life in the Philippines, designing and building magnificent government buildings, schools, hospitals, and homes.

Then it was all gone, reduced to rubble. He never spoke of it to me, but it must have broken his heart.

Closer to home, Mamita was worried about her house on Pennsylvania Avenue. As soon as it was safe I walked over with her, not knowing what to expect.

I was shocked by what I saw: all the homes were gone. What once had been a tree-lined street of stately homes was now littered with debris. The wrought iron fences were still in place, but there was nothing but rubble behind them. I was afraid to approach the site where I had spent so many happy days.

We stood at the fence and stared in silence, hands clutching the wrought iron stiles. I thought of Mamita's holy card collection and the porcelain frog orchestra, my heart sinking. I had been waiting so patiently for my sixteenth birthday, all in vain. I also recalled the big ugly spider whose web spanned the branches of the mango trees, but didn't mourn its loss.

The TES Uruguay

Mamita didn't have a key so we couldn't get past the gate. Perhaps that was best—to remember the beauty of what had been, and not to replace those memories with charred wood and melted silver like mom had experienced on Agno Street. We didn't speak much on the way home. I curled up in a quiet corner for a long while, deep in my own thoughts.

Papito was repatriated to the United States. He and Mamita were free to emigrate, provided they had a place to live. A woman living next door to Papito's sister in the Hollywood Hills was so short of cash that she was willing to live in the servants's quarters and rent out the house proper to my grandparents. They sailed for Los Angeles in May 1945.

Two months later we followed them. But not without some twists and turns in the road. As the daughter of a naturalized American citizen, Mom was also American, but her children were not, save Elaine, who was born after the Philippines became a commonwealth. Elyse and I were in legal limbo, aliens without a country. For a while it was unclear if U. S. Immigration would allow us to enter the States.

Eventually we came in under mom's passport. At age 21, Elyse and I had to pass the citizenship test and take the oath like any other immigrant. Because I had to earn it, I have always treasured my American citizenship.

In July 1945, Mom and her girls boarded the steamship *TES Uruguay* bound for San Francisco. Dad stayed behind to reestablish his businesses. As we walked up the gangplank, who did we see hanging out of a porthole, madly shouting and waving? Our old buddy Joe Barragan of the 1st Cavalry. Joe was one of the lucky ones being sent Stateside instead of to Okinawa. We were so happy to see him.

Our quarters were cramped—bunk beds stacked three high on either side of a narrow aisle. The four

Berg girls shared a cabin with a Russian woman and her young daughter. The woman was married to an American soldier, but hadn't seen or heard from him since the onset of war. She wasn't even sure if he was still alive. Mother and daughter were traveling to his parents's home to await word of his fate.

On board the *Uruguay* were over a thousand GIs and hundreds of civilian refugees. We were really packed in. Everyone got breakfast and dinner, but only kids were served lunch. I tasted my first peanut butter and jelly sandwich on that ship, and I got my fill. It seemed lunch was always PB&J, a glass of milk, and an apple. We saved some for mom, half a sandwich or an apple.

Elyse used her apples to barter with the servicemen for military patches and ribbons. She even acquired a Major's maple leaf insignia. By the time we reached San Francisco, she had a cigar box full of souvenirs.

Paying passengers were served fantastic dinners, on a par with the meals served nowadays on luxury cruise ships. The poor GIs, who had fought so valiantly for us, were treated to second-rate meals.

By day popular music was broadcast over the ship's loudspeakers. An on-board newspaper headlined the news and listed ship activities. Sometimes we were treated to talent shows on the ship's fantail.

Elyse and I had heard enough of the McGuire sisters by that time to lip sync some of their songs. If you're ever feeling blue, try performing for battle-weary GIs. It will do wonders for your self esteem—all that cheering and whistling!

When the ship's store opened in the morning the men lined up to buy cigarettes. By sheer coincidence Elyse and I happened to be around. Often we were treated to Butterfingers and Baby Ruths. We hadn't tasted either until then, and developed quite a liking for them. When our gentlemen friends didn't come through, mom gave us nickels to buy our own. The candy bars were huge, but I took teeny bites to make them last longer.

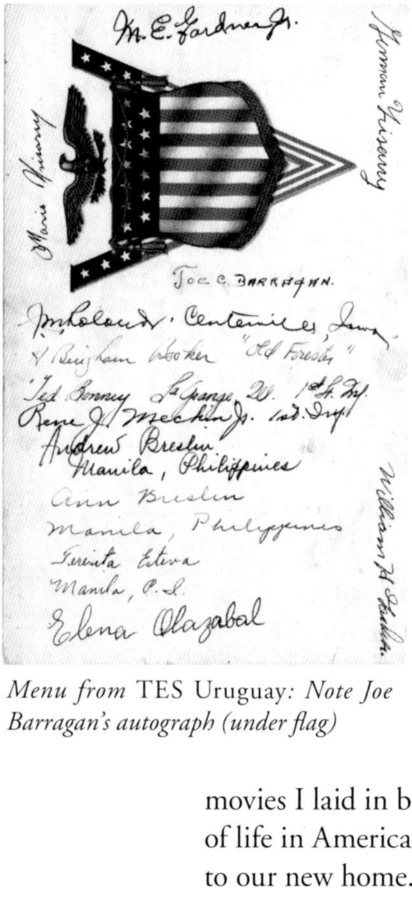

Menu from TES Uruguay*: Note Joe Barragan's autograph (under flag)*

Behind the backdrop of children playing was the ever-present threat of Japanese submarines. Destroyers were situated on either side of us. A mine sweeper trolled the seas ahead. We observed nightly blackouts and followed a zigzag course. The GIs were constantly reminded that even the light of a burning cigarette could prove fatal.

At night movies were shown behind heavy brocade draperies in the large dining hall. There were only a few films, so we saw the same ones over and over again. We loved them and didn't mind at all. After the movies I laid in bed and stared at the ceiling, dreaming of life in America. Each dawn brought us one day closer to our new home.

On August 6, Uncle Freddie's birthday, the music was interrupted by a news flash. The United States had dropped something called an atomic bomb on the Japanese city of Hiroshima. We all looked at each other, wondering what an atomic bomb was. Three days later another bomb was dropped on Nagasaki.

We steamed into Honolulu harbor to refuel and take on supplies. The skyline was dotted with palm and coconut trees, and a single pink hotel named the Royal Hawaiian. A far cry from the way it looks today.

The people in charge figured it would be next to impossible to round up the GIs once they had been let off the ship, so we all had to stay on board. We stood at the rail and gazed out at Waikiki beach and nearby Pearl Harbor. I thought back to December 7, four years earlier, and prayed for those who had lost their lives.

The Berg girls, Los Angeles, 1945 (from left): Elaine, Evelyn, and Elyse

After another week at sea, a blaring loudspeaker awakened us. Soon, the announcer said, we would be sailing into San Francisco Bay. Everyone scrambled on deck and rushed to the railing. There she was in all her glory, the magnificent Golden Gate Bridge, signifying freedom at last and a chance at the good life.

A few of the men started singing "California Here I Come." More and more joined in. Soon all were united in song, the power of their voices like a giant wave rolling over us. Tears streamed down the cheeks of even the most battle-hardened men. We cried too, but didn't sing along—we didn't know the words.

Late in the afternoon of August 13, 1945, with "God Bless America" and the National Anthem playing over the loudspeaker, our ship docked. We were in San Francisco—we were in America.

The following day Japan accepted terms of unconditional surrender.

LO QUE LOS OJOS HAN VISTO

EL CORAZÓN SE ACUERDA

Afterword

overleaf—title reads: "What the eyes have seen, the heart remembers"

General Tomoyuki Yamashita, wartime commander of Imperial Forces in the Philippines, was convicted of war crimes and hanged.

General Jonathan Wainwright was a prisoner of war until 1945. He was later awarded the Congressional Medal of Honor for heroism in the defense of Corregidor Island.

The American government, seeking to make an example of someone for collaboration with the enemy, investigated dad and members of the Aboitiz family. The Aboitiz clan owned a shipping company, and, like dad, had been forced to service and supply the Japanese Army.

After the initial Japanese invasion, General Douglas MacArthur and his family and staff had left Corregidor in the dark of night, bound for Bukidnon on the southern Philippine island of Mindanao. The propeller shaft on one of their PT boats snapped. The general's flotilla limped into the Aboitiz shipyard in neighboring Cebu for repairs, then continued on to the Del Monte plantation at Bukidnon, which had an airfield long enough to accommodate a B-17 bomber. The general's group was airlifted south across the Celebes Sea to safety in Australia.

The Aboitiz family received a Certificate of Commendation from the U. S. Government for aiding the general's escape.

Ernest Berg fared less well. He also had been forced to supply the Imperial Army, but because he was German was an easy target. *Guerrilla* pesos and receipts from the priest, his *guerrilla* contact, did him no good. After a summary investigation, Ernest was imprisoned. It is not clear he was even given a trial.

Manuel Roxas y Acuña, first president of the newly established Philippine Republic, released many political prisoners. Ernest was freed on July 6, 1946. He rebuilt Berg's department store one floor at a time, eventually restoring it to full operation, and reopened Red Star Auto Stores.

The Philippine government erected a memorial to Allied POWs at Cabanatuan. Fittingly it was designed in the shape of an inverted "V"—no victory...

The Manila Hotel, in which General MacArthur's headquarters had been housed at the start of the war, enshrined his quarters as a museum, including much of his memorabilia.

The German contingent of the Berg family survived the war in Europe. Except for Ernest's brother-in-law, a German army doctor who met his fate on a frozen battleground at the Russian front.

Lieutenant Katayama, Ernest's wartime nemesis, wrote to him from Japan in care of Berg Escolta. In the letter the lieutenant said that in the course of investigating Ernest he had acquired a great respect for him. Katayama asked for forgiveness, saying he had merely been doing his job. Ernest wrote back. A long-distance friendship was struck, and lasted a lifetime.

Ernest had originally purchased the country house in San Francisco del Monte as a place of safe retreat during the battle for the liberation of Manila. Ironically, toward the end of the war the family was unable to leave the city. Doubly ironic: staying in the city almost certainly saved their lives. The retreating Japanese Army burned down the country house and killed the servants. Ernest later built a house on that site for children orphaned in the war, and donated it to charity.

After moving to the United States, Ernest took his daughters on a summer tour of their new country. In every New Mexican town they visited they tried to locate Joe Barragan of the 1st Cavalry. As late as 1995, when Evelyn and her husband Richard spent Christmas in Albuquerque, three Barragans were listed in the local phone book. None was Joe, or knew of him.

Ernest's wrist, broken by Japanese interrogators at Ft Santiago, never properly healed. Of necessity he learned to type, pecking out his correspondence with his index fingers and scrawling his name at the bottom of the page. Despite his physical handicap, he later became an accomplished landscape painter.

In 1950, Ernest and Fé divorced. That same year, Ernest married Mimi Yak, his longtime secretary. They settled in Honolulu, Hawaii, and produced two children, Bonnie and Norman.

Ernest Berg with the author in Honolulu, 1971, a month before his death

Ernest, who dropped out of high school to support his family when his father died, earned a Ph.D. in Philosophy from the University of Hawaii.

Ernest Berg died in Honolulu in 1971, at the age of 70. At the funeral, there was a gorgeous bouquet of flowers by his casket. Evelyn asked Mimi who the flowers were from. She suggested that Evelyn read the attached card—it was from Lt Katayama.

After moving to Los Angeles, Fé, fearing that people would call her "Fee," changed the spelling of her name to "Fay."

Many times Fay was asked when she was going to buy another piano. She always gave the same answer: "We need too many things for the house." She never again played.

Elyse continued her dance lessons for several more years in Los Angeles under Madame Etienne. One of Elyse's fellow students was a girl named Mitzie Gerber, who went on to stage and movie fame as Mitzie Gaynor.

Dr Herbert Zipper and his wife Trudl Dubsky survived the war, and continued their careers in the United States. Dr Zipper was associated with the School of Performing Arts at the University of Southern California. An auditorium was later named in his honor.

The Berg family photographs were lost when the Agno Street house was destroyed. Fortunately Fay and her mother Carmen (Mamita) had religiously sent copies to Papito's family in Detroit. After moving to Los Angeles the photos were all returned.

Before the war, Ernest's brother Alfred met Helen Willkie, daughter of a U. S. Army officer stationed in Manila, and niece of Wendell Willkie, 1940 Republican presidential candidate. Alfred and Helen married and settled in Helen's native Kentucky. After her death around 1970, Alfred returned to Manila. There he became a successful importer of German cutlery and lived out the remainder of his days.

The Rodriguez family, today almost a hundred strong, emigrated to Madrid where Marcelino had been born.

The Tony Rocha family, half their original number, settled in America. They never again saw their neighbors, or their neighbor's pig.

The Aboitiz and Mari families remained in Manila, with two exceptions. Xavier "Xabi" Aboitiz attended Notre Dame University and later settled in Southern California. Tomas "Tomaset" Mari settled in Northern California.

Freddie and Carmen Mandelbaum and their daughter Carmencita settled in Southern California, where Frederick Jr later was born.

Dan Golenternek, Freddie's college chum, established a medical practice in Beverly Hills. Grateful for Freddie's friendship and help delivering medicines to the internment camp at Santo Tomas University, Dan delivered Frederick Jr free of charge.

Carmen and Cheri Mandelbaum, on their 50th wedding anniversary, April 30, 1958

In turn, Dr Golenternek delivered Evelyn's son, Stephen. The going rate in 1952 was $150, including the hospital.

When Evelyn's daughter Christine was little, Evelyn told her about how, after playing dolls or hosting tea parties, she would say to her *yah-yah*, Amalia, "Clean it up!" One day after Christine had finished playing with her Barbie dolls, she made a sweeping motion with her hand. Very seriously, she said, "Clean it up!" "Sorry, sweet child," Evelyn replied. "It doesn't work that way in Southern California."

Elyse Berg married and settled in Southern California. She has three children and four grandchildren.

Elaine Berg Ferry married and raised three children. She and her husband Don live on the Connecticut seacoast.

Francis "Cheri" Mandelbaum (Papito) died in Los Angeles in 1963, at the age of 92.

Carmen Romero Mandelbaum (Mamita) died in Los Angeles in 1976, at the age of 86.

In 1983, Evelyn returned to Manila with her husband Richard. There they visited the Oregon Street house. The banana tree in the front yard—beneath which Ernest had buried the slain Japanese officer—had grown up tall and strong.

That same trip Evelyn and Richard visited Corregidor Island, site of the Melinta Tunnel, where battle weary soldiers had been comforted by the beautiful woman the night before surrendering to the Japanese. Even decades later, visitors to the site often became so emotionally distraught that Japanese tourists were segregated on their own tour busses for fear of their safety.

Fay Mandelbaum Mugford remarried and settled in Sacramento, California. She died in Los Angeles in 1998, at the age of 88. Her jewelry, some of which had been hidden in Evelyn's Betsy Wetsy doll during the war, passed on to her daughters.

Appendices

Berg–Mandelbaum

Frederick Mandelbaum
1838 – 1876

Celina de Sourdis
1850 – 1915

Mathias Berg
died: c. 1915

Wilhelmina
Wiggers

Francis Cheri
Mandelbaum (Papito)
1871 – 1963

Ernest Berg
1901 – 1971

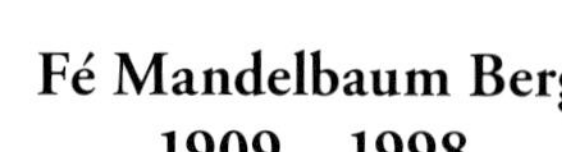

Fé Mandelbaum Berg
1909 – 1998

Evelyn Berg Empie
1931 –

Elyse Berg
1934 –

Elaine Berg Ferry
1938 –

Manuel Romero
died: c. 1895

Felisa G. Romero
died: c. 1936

Carmen Romero
Mandelbaum (Mamita)
1889 – 1976

Frederick "Freddie"
Mandelbaum
1915 –

Carmen Rickards
Mandelbaum
1918 –

Family Tree

*The Mandelbaum Residence,
1913 (from left) Fé Fannie,
Cheri, and Carmen*

Photographs

Celina de Sourdis Mandelbaum,
1850–1915

Frederick Mandelbaum, 1838–1876

The Mandelbaum residence on Calle de General Luna, Manila, Philippines, 1913

Fé Fannie Mandelbaum with her dog Pepe

Caption reads: "Love to you from Fe, Cheri and Carmen, Genoa, Italy, 8/8/1912"

Fé Fannie and Frederick Mandelbaum, c. 1918

The Mandelbaums at home, 1913

Carmen, Cheri, Frederick, and Fé Fannie, 1915

Evelyn Berg, 1932

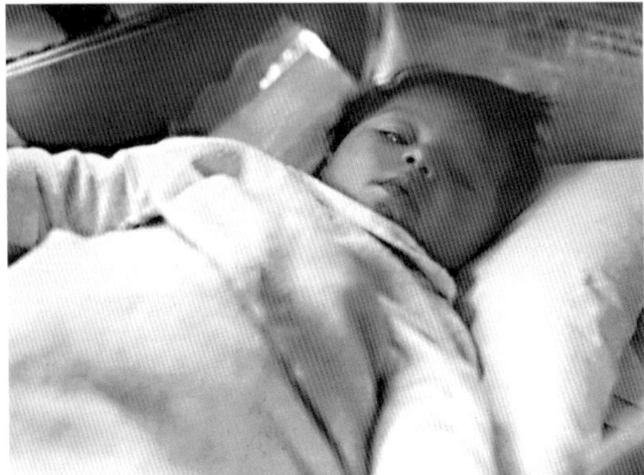

Elyse Berg, 1935

Fé and Ernest on their wedding day, May 27, 1929

Elaine Berg, 1939

Berg Escolta employee party, 1941, entertained by Shanghai's own Freddy Figueroa Swing Band

Elaine Berg

Elyse Berg

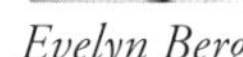

Evelyn Berg

Ernest Berg at work at Berg Escolta, 1940

"I shall carve

ATTENTION AMERICAN SOLDIERS!

I CEASE RESISTANCE

THIS LEAFLET GUARANTEES HUMANE TREATMENT TO ANY JAPANESE DESIRING TO CEASE RESISTANCE. TAKE HIM IMMEDIATELY TO YOUR NEAREST COMMISSIONED OFFICER.

By Direction of the Commander in Chief.

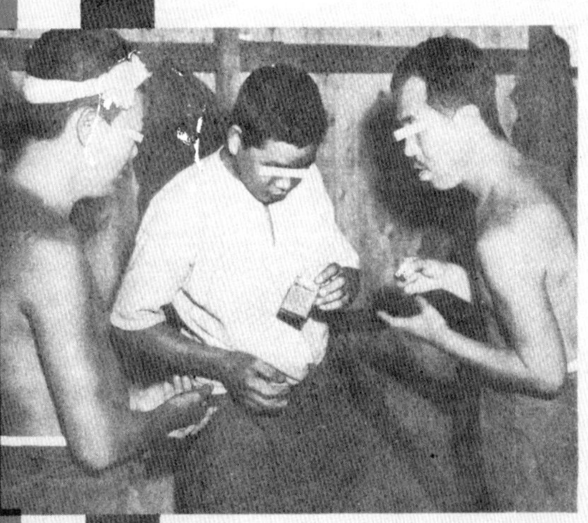

(日本の家族保護の為の目隠し)

上の英文の内容は「この人は最早敵でなく國際條約により生命、衣食住は勿論医療等が完全に保証さるべき者なり」と云ふ意味が書かれて居る
左圖は既に當方に来て居られる諸君の戰友の一部

17-J-1

an epitaph for you..."

A HANDSOME REWARD WILL BE YOURS

(1) if you capture an American parachutist and deliver him to the Japanese forces
(2) if you report any knowledge of spies in American service
(3) if you inform promptly of any movement of American troops, whether land, sea, or air forces.

THE JAPANESE FORCES IN THE PHILIPPINES

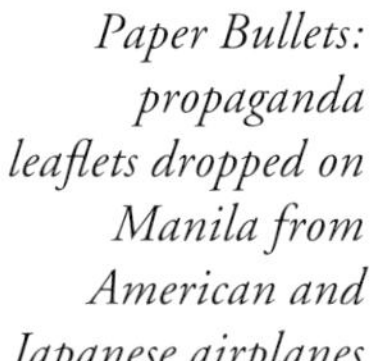

Paper Bullets: propaganda leaflets dropped on Manila from American and Japanese airplanes

FAREWELL, AMERICAN SOLDIERS!

You are still alive! What a miracle! And marching, too. But WHERE? To the Philippines? To Tokyo? But do you know what awaits you in the Philippines? Let me tell you. It is the Japanese forces with the combined support, both moral and material, of all the awakened Asiatics—the Manchukuoans, Chinese, Filipinos, Annamese, Thailanders, Burmese, Indians, Malayans and Indonesians. And the Japanese are there to pound you incessantly and relentlessly as you should have known. Perhaps they may retreat temporarily, but only to attack you again with double fierceness after your reinforcements have arrived. Day in and day out the Japanese troops are also pushing to the front in ever-increasing numbers. And remember, entire Asia is behind them! As long as you persist in marching west, the attacks will continue. Innumerable strongholds are all set to give you hearty welcome from the land, air and sea. The reverberation of their rousing welcome must even now be in your ears.

But this is not all. There is still another thing in store for you along the Philippines front. What is this thing? I will again answer you. It is a gravé, YOUR GRAVE! Nobody can say where it exactly is, but it is certain that it does exist somewhere in the Philippines, and you are bound to find it sooner or later, far or near. Today? Tomorrow? Who knows? But one thing is positive. You are heading west for your grave—as positive as the sun sets in the west. Officers and men, you still insist on marching west? If so, I shall have to carve an epitaph for you.

There are only two definite things on earth. LIFE and DEATH. The difference between LIFE and DEATH is absolute. One cannot rely upon the dead; no one can make friends with the dead; the dead can neither speak nor mingle with the living. If you insist on marching west, we (by we I mean all living things) must bid you goodbye and stop bothering with you, because we, the living, are too busy to have anything to do with the dead.

Your politicians are among those who survive and are enjoying life comfortably at home. General Marshall and General MacArthur can enjoy their reputation as heroes only because they are alive. But you... you continue to march westwards to sure death, to keep your rendesvous with the grave. The same holds true for your comrades-in-arms who are pathetically struggling to escape their ultimate fate. The graves await you, and you, and ALL OF YOU! So, officers and men, I bid you a pitiful goodbye. Today, you are with the living—tomorrow, with the dead. So again goodbye, American soldiers!...... Farewell!...... Farewell!......

"I have returned..."

GENERAL HEADQUARTERS
SOUTHWEST PACIFIC AREA
OFFICE OF THE COMMANDER-IN-CHIEF

PROCLAMATION

TO THE PEOPLE OF THE PHILIPPINES:

I have returned. By the grace of Almighty God our forces stand again on Philippine soil - soil consecrated in the blood of our two peoples. We have come, dedicated and committed, to the task of destroying every vestige of enemy control over your daily lives, and of restoring, upon a foundation of indestructible strength, the liberties of your people.

At my side is your President, Sergio Osmena, worthy successor of that great patriot, Manuel Quezon, with members of his cabinet. The seat of your government is now therefore firmly re-established on Philippine soil.

The hour of your redemption is here. Your patriots have demonstrated an unswerving and resolute devotion to the principles of freedom that challenges the best that is written on the pages of human history. I now call upon your supreme effort that the enemy may know from the temper of an aroused and outraged people within that he has a force there to contend with no less violent than is the force committed from without.

Rally to me. Let the indomitable spirit of Bataan and Corregidor lead on. As the lines of battle roll forward to bring you within the zone of operations, rise and strike. Strike at every favorable opportunity. For your homes and hearths, strike! For future generations of your sons and daughters, strike! In the name of your sacred dead, strike! Let no heart be faint. Let every arm be steeled. The guidance of divine God points the way. Follow in His Name to the Holy Grail of righteous victory!

Douglas MacArthur
DOUGLAS MacARTHUR.

Missive from Gen. Douglas MacArthur, distributed in Manila, 1944

Scenes of destruction: Manila, 1945...

Former site of Ayala Bridge on the Pasig River

Santa Rosa College

San Agustin Church

Site of Manila Cathedral

Inside the Walled City of historical Manila

Entrance to the Walled City, Manila

After the war: the family in Los

Elaine and Ernest Berg

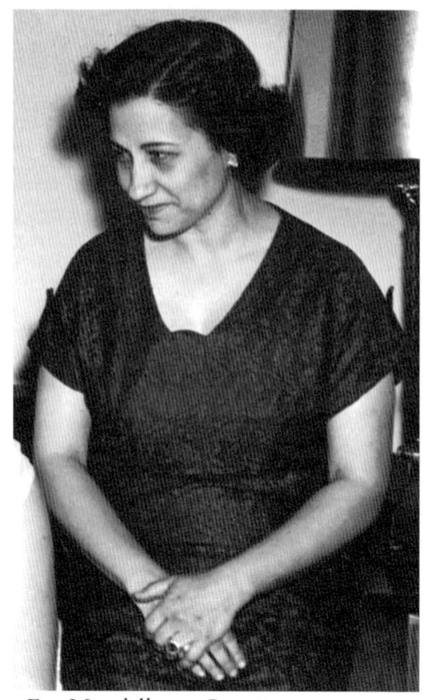

Fay Mandelbaum Berg

Elyse Berg

Evelyn Berg

Angeles

Elyse, Elaine, and Evelyn Berg

Cheri Mandelbaum with the co-author, Stephen H. Mette, 1952

Carmen and Cheri Mandelbaum, Los Angeles, 1948

Fay Mandelbaum Mugford in 1989, at her 80th birthday celebration

The Berg girls in 1989: (from left) Elyse Berg, Evelyn Berg Empie, Elaine Berg Ferry

Acknowledgments

A Child in the Midst of Battle comprises the collected memories of a young girl in a traumatic time, half a century hence. Any errors of fact or recollection are mine alone.

No book is written in isolation. Many thanks to my family and friends, without whose love and support this work would not exist.

To my husband Richard for his patience and encouragement.

To my daughter Christine M. Cramer, her husband Ron, and their children, Nathan, Timothy, and Elizabeth, for a constant love.

To my sisters, Elyse Berg and Elaine Berg Ferry. Thanks for the memories.

To my uncle Frederick Mandelbaum, his wife Carmen, and their children Carmencita Lostetter and Frederick Mandelbaum, for reminding me of details dimmed by time.

To my cousins, Gerardo "Lalo" Rodriguez, Lita Rocha, and Victoria "Mia" Trillo, and to my aunt's brother, Ralph "Chiqui" Rickards, for their generosity with their stories.

To my lifelong friends, Xavier "Xabi" and Rosalia Aboitiz, for their grace and humor. And for their memories.

To my longtime friends, Julie Perkins, Anita Bates, and Martha Delia Vazquez, for patiently urging me to record my experiences.

To Nicholas and Kimberly Empie, and their children Garrit and Whitney, I introduce a portion of my life of which they were not aware.

To Richard "Dick" Schouten and Eric Berryman of the World Ship Trust, for their tireless research.

To my son, Stephen H. Mette, the best writer I know, for his contribution to his family's history.

Lastly, perhaps most importantly, to the men and women of the U.S. Armed Forces, and especially the 1st Cavalry, for my liberation and for my life.

—Evelyn Berg Empie

To the above, I add special thanks to Evelyn and Richard Empie for their support.

To Xavier Aboitiz for the gracious use of his watercolors and drawings.

To Bernadette Shih, friend and fellow writer, for unwavering support and encouragement.

—Stephen H. Mette

About the Authors

Evelyn Berg Empie has five grandchildren. She lives in Southern California. This is her first book.

Stephen H. Mette is an award-winning poet. His previous work includes the novel *The Thanksgiving Trip*, and a volume of short fiction titled *Wild Life: and other adventures.* He lives in Southern California.

contact the authors at:

ebempie@hotmail.com
shmette@hotmail.com

Order Form

Post: Satori Press
904 Silver Spur Road #323
Rolling Hills Estates, CA 90274
USA
(Send photocopy of this form)

Tel: 310.377.1730

Please send the following titles:	Copies	x	Price	=	Amt.
A Child in the Midst of Battle	______	x	22.95	=	______
______	______	x	______	=	______
______	______	x	______	=	______

CA tax (8%, if applicable) $ ________

Shipping $ ________

Total $ ________

Shipping:

USA: $4.50 (US) for the first book
$2.50 (US) for each additional book

CAN: $7 (US) for the first book
$4 (US) for each additional book

Int'l: telephone, or email inquiries to shmette@hotmail.com

Name: ______________________________

Address: ______________________________

City: ____________________ State: ________ Zip: __________

Country: ____________ Telephone: ( ) ____________ email: ______________

Payment (US funds only): check or money order payable to Evelyn Empie